DIRECTIONS IN DE

CW00616207

The Transition from War to Peace in Sub-Saharan Africa

Nat J. Colletta
Markus Kostner
Ingo Wiederhofer

The World Bank
Washington, D.C.

In the cover panel are details from color woodcuts by Fred Mutebi, a Ugandan
artist who has exhibited in Africa and Europe. We are grateful to Mr. Mutebi
for granting permission to use these works.

Nat J. Colletta is head of the Post-Conflict Rapid Response Team in the World
Bank's Africa Region. Markus Kostner is a human resource economist, and
Ingo Wiederhofer is a demobilization and reintegration specialist; both are
consultants to the World Bank's Africa Technical Department.

Library of Congress Cataloging-in-Publication Data

Colletta, Nat J.
    The transition from war to peace in Sub-Saharan Africa / Nat J. Colletta,
Markus Kostner, Ingo Wiederhofer.
        p.   cm.— (Directions in development)
    Includes bibliographical references.
    ISBN 0-8213-3581-2
    1. Africa, Sub-Saharan—Economic policy.   2. Economic conversion—
Africa, Sub-Saharan.   3. Economic assistance—Africa, Sub-Saharan.
4. Manpower policy—Africa, Sub-Saharan.   I. Kostner, Markus.
II. Wiederhofer, Ingo, 1970–   .   III. Title.   IV. Series:
Directions in development (Washington, D.C.)
HC800.C6295   1996   96-10245
338.967—dc20   CIP

Contents

Foreword

The transition from war to peace and from economic crisis to revitalization is a fragile process characterized by intense political, economic, and ethnic rivalries. Nowhere is this transition more compelling, and nowhere are the rivalries more deeply rooted, than in Sub-Saharan Africa.

Although reported military expenditures in Sub-Saharan Africa, excluding South Africa, have declined significantly (from $3.5 billion in 1987 to $1.9 billion in 1993), poverty, inequality, and ethnic discrimination continue to foster conflict and undermine the authority of several African states. The resulting fragmentation has led to an alarming privatization of violence: armed bands, often aligned with political, ethnic, and other special interests, rush to fill the vacuum left by a diminished state security and administrative apparatus. Indeed, fragmentation and violence threaten the very existence of some African states, such as Somalia and Liberia.

This weakening of the overall security umbrella that had readily received external financing during the cold war has produced a flood of displaced people and refugees. In Central and Eastern Africa alone, about 22 million people are displaced (within the country or externally). Natural disasters and famine used to be the root of human suffering and displacement in Africa; now, internal conflict is the leading cause of emergencies in many countries.

The convergence of a decade of economic deterioration with the end of the cold war has created a climate in which a growing number of African governments, whether emerging from internal conflict or at peace, are exploring ways to address persistent poverty by reallocating scarce resources from military budgets. In this changing context, demobilization and reintegration programs (DRPs) for military personnel constitute the central element of the transition from war to peace. DRPs not only provide assistance to an especially vulnerable and potentially volatile group among the poor; they also help rebuild a secure foundation on which an economy can grow sustainably.

Several countries have asked the donor community, including the World Bank, to provide technical assistance and financing for demobilization and reintegration efforts. In response, the World Bank's Africa Regional Office has adopted a two-pronged strategy: first, it established, in 1992, a working group to examine the African experience with DRPs and to assess the potential role of the Bank, and second, it began to offer technical and financial assistance to those governments that sought help in the design and implementation of DRPs.

The efforts of the working group culminated in the Africa Regional Discussion Paper "Demobilization and Reintegration of Military Personnel in Africa: The Evidence from Seven Country Case Studies" (World Bank 1993). The study, which was based on secondary data, focused on design issues of the demobilization phase and identified the key factors that influence the outcome of a DRP. The report found a wide audience among client governments, donors, United Nations agencies, nongovernmental organizations, and academics.

Concurrently, the Bank provided technical and financial assistance to the governments of Mozambique, Rwanda, and Uganda. In Uganda the Bank played a central role in the development and implementation of a program that, over the past three years, has reduced defense expenditures from 35 to 25 percent of the current national budget and has cut the size of the army almost in half, from 80,000 to 43,000 soldiers. The Bank also assisted in the design of a DRP for Rwanda, but the tragic turn of internal political events and the ensuing change of government preempted the program. Recently, the government of Rwanda has again requested the Bank's leadership in DRP design. This time, social reconciliation will be part of the overall program. Current assistance to Mozambique focuses primarily on reintegration, with an emphasis on generating employment and training through support for microprojects and through capacity building. This program has been recently expanded to target displaced persons and returning refugees, as well as ex-combatants.

Other DRPs have been substantially completed (Chad and Zimbabwe) or are well on their way to completion (Eritrea and Ethiopia). Many more African countries—for example, Angola, Djibouti, Liberia, Sierra Leone, South Africa, and Togo—have emerged as potential candidates for DRP assistance, as have Bosnia, Cambodia, and Sri Lanka outside Africa. Finally, DRPs for Somalia and the Sudan will most likely materialize in the more distant future.

The growing experience with DRPs has helped the Bank to crystallize a number of key policy and programmatic issues. These include targeting criteria and mechanisms, program options, costs and effectiveness, institutional arrangements for implementation, restoration of social capital, economic impact (the "peace dividend"), and donor coordination.

In order to fill gaps in knowledge and to assist client governments, international partners (multilateral and bilateral agencies and nongovernmental organizations), and Bank staff in improving the design and implementation of DRPs, the Africa Regional Office prepared a "best practices" study focusing on the reinsertion and reintegration of ex-combatants. The study, to be issued as a World Bank Discussion Paper (Colletta and others forthcoming), draws on the lessons learned from in-depth country studies of Ethiopia, Namibia, and Uganda. The experiences of these countries offer an extensive range of social, political, and economic contexts and program models and contain a wide variety of important lessons.

This book, which is based on the "best practices" paper and supporting country studies, provides a window on the complex political, economic, and sociocultural transitions that face many countries. These insights will be shared with our clients and our partners as we work together toward enduring peace and prosperity on the African continent.

E. V. K. Jaycox
Vice President
Africa Regional Office
The World Bank

March 1996

Preface

Africa was among the first battlefronts and final casualties of the cold war. Many devastating conflicts have persisted for twenty years or more. Some countries (such as Ethiopia, Namibia, South Africa, Uganda, and, more recently, Angola and Mozambique) are emerging from years of cold war politics and internal civil strife, but pernicious internal struggles continue to plague others (Liberia, Somalia, and the Sudan, for example).

The damage inflicted on the social capital and economic potential of these countries has been horrific. Of the estimated 80 million to 110 million land mines spread across 64 countries around the world, about 20 million are strewn across nearly half the countries of Africa. The impact of warfare on disinvestment, the destruction of physical infrastructure, and the deterioration of human capital through disability, death, and displacement is impossible to quantify. However, armed conflict is surely one reason why at least 250 million people in Sub-Saharan Africa—nearly half the population—are living below the poverty line in the mid-1990s.

While war-ravaged countries are among the poorest in the world, their neighbors, in which hundreds of thousands of people seek refuge from the devastation of war, are often in no better position. Over the past decade the African continent hosted about half of the world's displaced people, and by 1994, 21.4 million Africans had fled their homes because of conflict. Of these, 6.2 million were living abroad, representing 38 percent of the world's refugees.

Despite these dire circumstances, the governments of the continent have devoted a substantial percentage of gross domestic product (GDP) to military expenditures (3.1 percent in 1992). Expenditures for defense have crowded out those for human development; in many countries in Sub-Saharan Africa they surpass expenditures for health and education combined.

The ideological camps that once fueled military buildups receded with the end of the cold war, making it possible for many African governments to downsize their militaries and reduce defense expenditures so that human and material resources may be shifted to development activities. Demobilization and reintegration programs for military personnel constitute a vital part of demilitarization in general, and of transitions from war to peace in particular.

Indeed, increased demilitarization is a precondition for reviving civil society, reducing poverty, and sustaining development in Africa. The realization of this objective demands disarmament, demining, and demobilization of forces, as well as the reintegration of ex-combatants into productive civilian roles. Demilitarization also requires the reduction of the destructive flow of arms into the continent.

World suppliers of arms continue to sell large quantities of military hardware to Sub-Saharan Africa, and this could be an obstacle to a rapid transition to peace. In the past, principals in the cold war armed local factions or entire countries; internal factions now rely on the control and sale of precious natural resources (ranging from forest woods to diamonds and oil) to sustain their arms purchases. The path to peace on the continent is thus littered with mines, both underground and in the form of violent sociopolitical rivalry.

The millions of displaced people scattered within and around the borders of warring countries are a grim reminder of the human consequences of such conflicts. The relationship between poverty and conflict is clear. What an Africa unblemished by internal conflicts would have looked like is hard to imagine.

Rationale and Objectives

As with civil service reform, reductions in military forces can yield great dividends for budgetary reallocations. These dividends constitute an important economic rationale for embarking on a demobilization program, particularly in peacetime. Furthermore, by reducing arms procurement and building security, DRPs have an overarching impact on fiscal policy, investment behavior, formulation of policy in the social sectors, and related poverty reduction efforts.

In war-torn societies, the demobilization and reintegration of ex-combatants are integral parts of the political-military solution to conflict, and DRPs lie at the heart of transition from war to peace. It is the key instrument for moving beyond humanitarian assistance to poverty reduction and sustainable reconstruction. DRPs, however, are highly complex operations that often affect more people from a lower human capital and asset base (the poorer segments of society) than does civil service reform.

The principal objective of this book is to inform Bank management and staff, client governments, international organizations, and nongovernmental organizations (NGOs) about best practices for improving the design and implementation of programs for demobilization, reinsertion, and reintegration in client countries. Identifying high-impact, cost-effective program options and design features on the basis of experience is important for the success of DRP operations both in peacetime and in transitions from war to peace.

This book also provides early warning signals of what can go wrong in the DRP process and suggests preventive actions. Intentionally, however, it does not offer a blueprint for universal application because such a generalized prescription cannot substitute for a thorough understanding of the political, social, and economic conditions and needs in a given country. Only such comprehensive knowledge can lead to an in-depth, country-specific design process with good prospects for success.

Because DRPS address broad issues of populations in transition, they may also hold valuable lessons for projects that support the economic and social reintegration of other vulnerable groups, such as repatriated refugees, internally displaced populations, retrenched civil servants, and former employees of privatized parastatals. Such projects might focus on generic reinsertion and reintegration activities that include the provision of safety nets, information, counseling, and referral services, resettlement schemes, credit and business advice, and retraining and employment programs.

Methodology

The research followed multiple approaches: collection of secondary data that have become available since completion of the first DRP study; incorporation of primary data involving new information at the administrative and field levels; and the authors' direct field visits and experience in DRP design work. Two assessments of the impact of DRPs—one quantitative, the other qualitative—were commissioned in Ethiopia and Namibia and undertaken by local researchers. In Ethiopia sixteen communities were assessed, and in Namibia interviews were held in twelve communities. In addition, the program monitoring and evaluation system provided an in-depth assessment of thirteen communities in Uganda.

All impact assessments were based on purposive sampling and triangulation of responses from the three groups most affected by the program: ex-combatants, family members, and community members. The field visits also captured the reflections of program staff.

Even at this stage, some gaps in knowledge exist. As a result of the emergency nature of the programs, especially those in Ethiopia and Namibia, these gaps can never be completely filled. The dual approach of the research strategy nevertheless supplies information that is sufficiently robust for drawing lessons and making cross-country comparisons. We hope that the book will help improve the design and implementation of future DRPs in Sub-Saharan Africa and other regions.

Acknowledgments

This book has benefited from considerable input from colleagues both within and outside the Bank. It is based in part on in-depth field analysis of demobilization and reintegration in Ethiopia, Namibia, and Uganda. Those three country studies, prepared with the assistance of Emilio Mondo, Taimi Sitari, and Tadesse A. Woldu, are being published as a World Bank Discussion Paper, *Case Studies in War-to-Peace Transition: The Demobilization and Reintegration of Ex-Combatants in Ethiopia, Namibia, and Uganda.*

The book would not have been possible without the extraordinary openness and collaboration of the Ethiopian Commission for the Rehabilitation of Members of the Former Army and Disabled War Veterans; the Namibian Ministry of Lands, Resettlement and Rehabilitation; the Namibian Development Brigade Corporation; and the Uganda Veterans Assistance Board. We would also like to thank the Swiss government, which provided a grant to finance the overall project, and the U.S. Agency for International Development, which cofinanced the Ethiopian field study.

Special thanks for comments and suggestions are owed to the members of the Africa Regional Working Group on Demobilization: Nicolas Gorjestani, Philippe Benoit, Laura Frigenti, Sarah Keener, Elisabeth Morris-Hughes, Luiz Pereira da Silva, Sanjay Pradhan, and Bension Varon.

Also appreciated are comments and support from Kevin Cleaver, Katherine Marshall, Jean-Louis Sarbib, Ishrat Husain, Peter Miovic, Jack van Holst Pellekan, Fayez Omar, Steven Adei, Esther Hoveka, Bruce Schimming, Brian Falconer, Hasan Imam, Ritva Reinikka, Hyoungsoo Zang, Charles Mordi, Mimi Klutstein-Meyer, Ashton Douglass, Kerstin Wilde, Dawit Eshetu, Chukwuma Obidegwu, Loganathan Kanagasabai, Iradj Alikhani, and Elizabeth Acul.

The final version of the book was edited by Donna Daniels Verdier. Abigail Tardiff was the proofreader.

Summary and Lessons

In his speech at the 1995 annual meetings of the World Bank and the International Monetary Fund, James Wolfensohn, president of the World Bank, declared that a priority of the Bank is to anticipate and be organized for postconflict economic development programs. A demobilization and reintegration program (DRP) for ex-combatants is the key to an effective transition from war to peace. The success of this first step following the signing of a peace accord signals the end to organized conflict and provides the security necessary for people affected by war to reinvest in their lives and their country.

Reinsertion and reintegration are not distinct phases after demobilization. Rather, they form part of a seamless web of transition from military to civilian life, without a clear beginning or end. As reinsertion and reintegration proceed, the needs of ex-combatants change and call for different support measures.

A successful DRP requires several actions: (a) classifying ex-combatants according to their characteristics, needs and desired way of earning a livelihood (mode of subsistence); (b) offering a basic transitional assistance package (safety net); (c) finding a way to deliver assistance simply, minimizing transaction costs while maximizing benefits to ex-combatants; (d) providing counseling, information, training, employment, and social support while sensitizing communities and building on existing social capital; (e) coordinating centrally yet decentralizing implementation authority to districts; and (f) connecting to ongoing development efforts by retargeting and restructuring existing portfolios.

This book examines ways to determine the impact of a DRP on ex-combatants. The key lessons drawn from this examination warrant close consideration by Bank staff, client governments, donors, and nongovernmental organizations (NGOs) involved in the design and implementation of DRPs. These lessons are summarized below and are discussed in greater detail in subsequent chapters.

Political Dimensions

When a country is moving from war to peace, demobilization and reintegration issues should be addressed at the earliest stages of the peace negotiation process. Strong political will and leadership, expressed in

1

terms of commitment, realism, and pragmatism, are crucial factors for successful program implementation.

National reconciliation should be actively promoted through transparent policies and conflict resolution efforts at the community level. These can reduce suspicion and help rebuild trust.

The question of land ownership and distribution needs to be treated carefully and openly. Both traditional and legal rights to the land, as well as historically rooted inequalities, have to be taken into account.

Targeting

Ex-combatants constitute a specially vulnerable group in need of priority targeted assistance. Socioeconomic data should be collected to reveal their characteristics, needs, and aspirations so that appropriate program interventions can be designed.

Careful analysis of the opportunity structure for ex-combatants (in particular, the demand for labor and the availability of land, credit, information, and provision for skill development) is a prerequisite not only for program design but also for targeted counseling and adequate placement.

An authentic, nontransferable, and noncorruptible identification system is of paramount importance for avoiding targeting errors.

The particular challenges confronting veterans' dependents (the family), as well as female soldiers, child soldiers, and disabled ex-combatants, warrant the development of specially targeted interventions.

Demobilization

Ex-combatants should be released or discharged from military quarters as soon as possible so that they do not become a serious threat to security. Prior to discharge, they should receive information about civilian life—rights and duties, opportunities and constraints. If feasible, postdischarge orientation, with a focus on social support and economic opportunities, should be provided in the communities where ex-combatants settle.

Especially in transitions from war to peace, neutral international monitors and technical assistance can facilitate the design and implementation of demobilization programs.

Reinsertion

Entitlement packages, which provide a safety net during the transition from war to peace, should reflect the needs of ex-combatants and their families in different socioeconomic environments. Such packages help ex-combatants and their families bridge the difficult period between demobilization and reintegration.

Monetizing the entitlement packages has several advantages over in-kind provision: transaction costs can be reduced, leakage can be better controlled, and beneficiaries can make flexible use of the entitlement.

Using local banks for transferring cash in installments allows ex-combatants to access financial assistance throughout the reinsertion phase. Staggered payments made to beneficiaries through local banks also help spread benefits and ex-combatants throughout the country. The capacity of the banking system or alternate payment systems, especially in rural areas, must therefore be evaluated before transfers begin.

Reintegration

Ex-combatants should be assigned to target groups and subgroups on the basis of their mode of subsistence and thus on their differing needs and aspirations. This allows for the development of a differentiated, relevant, and cost-effective approach.

Ex-combatants should receive no more support than is necessary to help them attain the standard of living of the communities into which they are reintegrated.

Reintegration in urban areas is more complex than in rural areas and requires a more diversified approach. All support measures should be based on a careful matching of opportunities and actual needs. Support measures should, to the extent possible, be demand-driven.

Social Dimensions

It is the interplay of a community's physical and social capital and the ex-combatant's financial and human capital that ultimately determines the ease and success of reintegration.

Efforts to strengthen social capital—for example, by using existing community organizations and channels of communication—enable communities to take development into their own hands and facilitate reintegration of ex-combatants.

Informal networks of ex-combatants—discussion groups, veterans' associations, and joint economic ventures—are key elements for successful economic and social reintegration. Such associations can be extremely helpful when social capital has been depleted.

A community support program that provides visible benefits to the community is a critical adjunct to assistance for ex-combatants.

Community sensitization and political awareness are paramount in this effort.

Care should be taken that ex-combatants are not stigmatized as unfit for military service or as conveyors of disease, violence, and misbehavior.

Institutional Concerns

To put scarce resources to optimal use, program components should be ranked by simplicity of implementation, with the simplest components first on the list.

Central coordination of DRPs by one civilian agency with overall responsibility, balanced by decentralization of implementation authority to districts and communities through existing organizational structures, makes for a powerful institutional arrangement.

Administrative costs need to be held down. The higher the transaction (administrative) costs, the smaller the resources available to ex-combatants.

The effectiveness of program interventions in relation to ongoing development initiatives is maximized by careful coordination within government and among other project promoters.

Once the major program objectives have been fulfilled, remaining activities should be integrated into the government's mainstream development efforts.

Elected representatives of ex-combatants, as well as field-based staff, can perform crucial roles in facilitating reintegration.

Local communities should be involved directly in decisionmaking, especially on important local matters, so that scarce public resources are allocated in a transparent and socially accountable manner.

Management Aspects

Staff training to improve skills and knowledge should begin before demobilization and should emphasize practical problem solving.

The most important contribution of a monitoring and evaluation system is to consistently improve ongoing operations—by keeping abreast of major trends in the program and by regularly reporting to and advising management.

Use of an external auditor improves management of funds. The external auditor, in addition to ensuring control of program resources and transparency, gives confidence to the donors and to the beneficiaries.

External Assistance

Timely availability of resources facilitates smooth operations. Donor budget cycles and disbursement and auditing procedures have to be closely meshed with implementation schedules for DRPs.

Capacity building and close coordination among the government, NGOs, community-based groups, and donors are central elements of cooperation. Coordination of donor support by a lead donor has proved very effective.

Economic Impact

The peace dividend needs to be understood in social and economic terms, as well as in financial terms. The reinvestment of some savings from military downsizing into the development of a disciplined, high-quality defense force can itself produce a peace dividend by increasing security, building confidence, and reducing public fear.

It is useful to link a country's overall macroeconomic reform program, especially as it concerns the public expenditure mix, to the planned reintegration program.

Jump-starting the economy by rehabilitating critical infrastructure also can be linked to reintegration programs that involve training and employment schemes for both reconstructing material assets and building human and social capital.

Continental demilitarization is a precondition for reviving civil society, reducing poverty, and sustaining development in Africa. The realization of this objective hinges on disarmament, the demobilization of forces, and the reduction of the flow of arms into the continent, on the one hand, and on the reintegration of ex-combatants into productive civilian roles, on the other.

Revitalizing civil society entails the promotion of local associations, community participation, and peer accountability, all of which reduce individual fear, enable collective condemnation of violence, and strengthen local security. These are the minimal conditions for encouraging people to reinvest in their communities both emotionally and financially.

1
Designing a DRP: Best Practices

Demobilization and reintegration programs are complex operations with overlapping and interdependent phases, crosscutting issues, and many participants. This chapter addresses the structure of a DRP. First, the *political dimensions* establish the fundamental preconditions on which a program needs to be built. With the help of targeting, the numbers and particulars of ex-combatants—and therefore the magnitude of the problem and program—can be identified. This in turn furnishes the basis for the design of demobilization, reinsertion, and reintegration, the three interdependent processes in the transition from military to civilian life.

Political Will: A Fundamental Precondition

Demobilization and reintegration programs take place in specific social and political contexts at several levels: the state, the community, the family, and the demobilized ex-combatants themselves are all affected. It is of paramount importance that demobilization and reintegration be addressed appropriately and adequately during the peace process. Involving development agencies early in this process is advantageous for linking relief to development.

Where the conflict results in a standoff with no apparent victor, mediation by a third party or by the United Nations is required. In such circumstances a critical political dimension of the peace process is usually the global incorporation of the military forces of the warring parties into a single security force (police and army). Ironing out the details of a combined security force can be tedious, but the peace agreement must address the issue comprehensively lest it remain a nagging obstacle to swift demobilization and reintegration.

Conflict-related demobilization efforts commonly involve more politicization, sensitivity, and uncertainty than do peacetime DRPs, especially when there is no clear victor. In this context, the success of a DRP depends on the political commitment of the parties to the peace process. However, by the same token, the success or failure of the DRP can determine the fate of that process.

For example, although the Angolan DRP of 1993 failed primarily because one side refused to accept defeat in the national elections and resumed its armed struggle, poor monitoring and management of the demobilization process by the international community may have contributed to insecurity. Strong political leadership on the part of all political and warring factions—as reflected in commitment, realism, and pragmatism—is thus a crucial factor for successful design and implementation of DRPs.

Beyond such national political issues, regional security developments can promote or undermine a DRP. For example, the deterioration in relations between Sudan and Eritrea has delayed completion of the demobilization process in the latter. Similarly, increasing security concerns on Uganda's northern border have forced the remobilization of some Ugandan ex-combatants into home guards and local defense units, and conflicts in Liberia and Sierra Leone are linked by armies that know no borders.

DRP planning can be initiated before a peace accord is signed. In fact, assistance is more likely to be timely if preparations for the DRP are made during the ceasefire or when a lasting accord seems within reach. Such efforts are warranted even if they turn out to be in vain in the short term (as in Rwanda in 1994). At the very least, they provide critical design information and serve as an incentive for ending the struggle when an exit strategy does materialize.

The reinsertion and reintegration of demobilized combatants take place in social and cultural environments that determine their constraints and opportunities. When social capital has been eroded and ethnic or regional tensions prevail, reinsertion and reintegration are far more complex and difficult to achieve. For example, Ugandan ex-combatants were generally well received by communities in the center and southwest of the country, where the National Resistance Movement had its support base, but those attempting to resettle in the east of the country initially faced community hostility. In Namibia some Ovambo ex-combatants who fought on the losing side faced resentment on their return to the northern part of the country.

The demobilization of soldiers, especially in peacetime, is clearly in the interest of the army command if living conditions and wages for remaining military personnel are thereby improved. Demobilization and increases in army efficiency (including modernization) are two sides of the same coin. Although assisting armies is not within the purview of development agencies (bilateral or multilateral), the legitimate interest of the government in establishing a functioning security apparatus must be taken into account even if part of the budgetary savings from the demobilization accrues in the short term to a leaner, more disciplined military. Ultimately, the effectiveness of a DRP will depend on mutual trust between government and donors and, consequently, on the degree of good governance.

Ex-combatants, who can potentially destabilize a country but who also share many characteristics of the poor population at large, can justifiably be treated as a special target group for receiving priority government support. Despite their special status, ex-combatants should not receive preferential treatment over other vulnerable groups, if at all possible. Instead, ongoing government, donor, and NGO programs should be incorporated into the design of the DRP.

For example, ex-combatants in Ethiopia received food from the Ethiopian Red Cross Society and the Relief and Rehabilitation Commission under those organizations' mandate to supply food to returning refugee families. Such arrangements can ease reintegration pressure on ex-combatants and reduce transaction costs. To lessen community resentment, the program should enhance community development and be well publicized. Any unwarranted negative publicity should be addressed professionally through press releases or radio broadcasting.

Well-conceived programs that address these issues can contribute significantly to political and ethnic reconciliation, rehabilitation of the economic base, and restoration of social capital at the community level. The peace dividend of a DRP therefore needs to be understood in broader social and economic terms as well as in financial terms.

Targeting: The Central Element

Three steps have to be completed to ensure that a DRP is targeted effectively: the primary and secondary beneficiaries need to be identified on the basis of specific criteria; needs and opportunities have to be ascertained; and an effective targeting mechanism must be developed.

Identification of Beneficiaries

Ex-combatants are the primary beneficiaries of a DRP. The criteria for their selection should be transparent in order to avoid discrimination by ethnicity, region, or gender. Identifying ex-combatants for demobilization can be difficult. If they are to be demobilized from a regular army, army records (certificates of service or salary statements, for instance) can be consulted, although such data are normally confidential. If, as is likely for guerrilla forces, such records do not exist, other methods have to be employed.

In the absence of official records, comrades' committees, which include former commanding officers, may be the most effective source of information, especially when combatants are not assembled in camps but report individually. The role of these committees should be limited to verifying that an individual was indeed a combatant; the committees should not be charged with other activities such as the verification of an individual's employment status. Receipts issued to ex-combatants when they turn in their weapons to the government, the victorious army, or United Nations agencies are other indicators of ex-combatant status. Finally, combatants can be encamped with the specific purpose of establishing their numbers and particulars. Special encampment also helps eliminate "ghost soldiers" from payroll rosters. Once combatants have been identified, it is the responsibility of the army high command to determine which of them are to be demobilized.

Every effort should be undertaken to register all ex-combatants properly and ensure equal treatment; inconsistencies in registration reverberate throughout program implementation. Likewise, the particulars of each ex-combatant should be recorded accurately. For example, the rank of soldiers should not be inflated, especially if benefits vary by rank; rank inflation leads to disparities, discontent, and higher costs than necessary. Furthermore, combatants of defeated armies have to be assured that registration will not expose them to retribution, persecution, or extralegal punitive action.

Although ex-combatants are the immediate target group of a DRP, their discharge has significant implications for their families and communities. If the DRP will include spouses and children as beneficiaries, ex-combatants should be asked to identify these family members prior to discharge. It is useful to specify the family's community of settlement in advance because some communities are likely to be affected more than others. Consequently, all relevant communities may receive some support.

Identification of Needs and Opportunities

Appropriate program design requires information in three areas: the supply side (the characteristics, needs, and aspirations of ex-combatants); the demand side (the opportunities and constraints that ex-combatants will face when they enter the labor market as employees or as self-employed workers); and the social environment to which ex-combatants will return. Preparatory studies are therefore crucial to success. These should typically includes analysis of the socioeconomic profile of ex-combatants, the opportunity structure, the social capital of the community, and the institutional structure necessary to implement the program.

SOCIOECONOMIC PROFILE. Information on ex-combatants is best collected while they are still in camps or barracks. The sample survey (or census) must include data on demographics, health status, educational attainments, access to resources (land, capital, and other assets), work experience, original location and desired place of relocation, and planned occupation after demobilization. If those who are to be demobilized have not yet been identified, care should be taken to ensure that ex-combatants do not associate the fact of having been interviewed with their possible demobilization. The information gathered provides the basis for a socioeconomic profile of the ex-combatants.

The socioeconomic profile may not vary much among countries. Most ex-combatants share many of the characteristics of the country's poor population: they tend to be illiterate, or functionally so; they are probably in poor health; they have few or no nonmilitary skills; they may have lost their entire family and thus their immediate social network; and they have little capital, few assets, and limited access to land. In addition, ex-combatants have adapted to a military command structure and often find it difficult to make decisions independently.

In some countries, many ex-combatants may be infected with the HIV virus or other communicable disease, which could be spread throughout the country. Wives and female ex-combatants often face particular social constraints and expectations, as do child soldiers, who often know nothing of civilian life. Finally, the disabled may be perceived very differently in different societies. In short, most ex-combatants belong to an especially vulnerable group in need of priority assistance. The public needs to be educated about their needs and capabilities.

The socioeconomic profile could be used to categorize ex-combatant beneficiaries into the following subgroups: rural and urban mode of subsistence, female ex-combatants, child soldiers, disabled ex-combatants, longer-serving ex-combatants, pensioners, and the especially vulnerable (such as ethnic minorities). Those who were conscripted or served for only a short time may not need specific reintegration support, but they may still require assistance with reinsertion.

If necessary, these subgroups can be disaggregated further. For instance, the disabled can be categorized as less severely, moderately, or more severely disabled. Within each of these subgroups, ex-combatants from either faction should receive equal treatment, unless the terms and conditions of service differ explicitly. Multiple support strategies based on such categorization could be designed to be mutually reinforcing and could be presented as a needs-based, differentiated, relevant, and cost-effective menu-style approach.

OPPORTUNITY STRUCTURE. The study of the opportunity structure would enable planners to identify those areas of intervention with the highest absorptive capacity. This study would analyze various markets, such as land, labor, credit, skills development, information, and technology. Its aim would be to identify the opportunities for market access (reinsertion) open to beneficiaries. Such reinsertion opportunities could then be matched with ex-combatants' needs and aspirations through counseling, information, and referral mechanisms to smooth the transition to a productive civilian life.

SOCIAL CAPITAL. The study on social capital would assess the cohesiveness of communities, the communities' levels of interpersonal trust, their potential for active participation in program implementation, their attitude toward the broader issue of national reconciliation, and their capacity to act as support networks. Combined with the regional distribution of ex-combatants after demobilization, this study would also identify the need to target special program assistance to communities.

Ideally, detailed results from all studies would be available before the DRP was designed. In practice, however, time constraints may preclude completion of full-fledged studies. In such circumstances a preliminary profile can be prepared on the basis of data gathered in focus group interviews conducted during encampment and merged with general information on countrywide economic development. Concurrently, a rapid qualitative assessment of the community and organizational structures can be undertaken.

In principle, the survey of ex-combatants could include the identification of the needs of spouses and children, even though ex-combatants may not be able to report accurately on the needs of their family members. A full-fledged survey of these secondary target groups is likely to be expensive and time consuming. It may therefore be necessary to develop certain program interventions on the basis of evidence about the poor population at large; recent household survey data might be one source for that evidence.

Development of an Effective Target Mechanism

Once ex-combatants have been identified, they need to be issued nontransferable and noncorruptible identification documents. A discharge certificate specifying the particulars of the ex-combatant (including a photograph and signature or thumbprint) and outlining entitlements may be the simplest way for ex-combatants to access program benefits. If benefits are to be transferable (on death, for example), a section on the rights of next-of-kin would have to be included. The certificate should be designed to be durable and easily portable. Documents for particular subtarget groups may also be issued (for example, community verification letters for family members, or disability cards). Community committees may be helpful in identifying needy ex-combatants.

The purpose of such identification documents is twofold: to enable eligible ex-combatants to draw benefits, and to ensure that no one other than ex-combatants and their spouses and children receive benefits (that is, to avoid leakage). To this end, a clear procedure for replacing lost or stolen certificates has to be developed.

Effective program implementation is just as important as a well-developed targeting mechanism. Especially where two or more opposing armies are to be demobilized, every effort must be made to preclude any ethnic or political bias by program staff. Moreover, the greater the number of institutions involved in implementation, the closer their activities need to be coordinated to avoid targeting errors and duplication. The institutional structure for implementation should be kept lean by building on existing structures, rather than create new bureaucracies.

Demobilization: The Essential First Step

Demobilization is the first part of the DRP process that a combatant passes through. It consists of the following segments: cantonment (sometimes termed "assembly" or "quartering"), predischarge orientation, discharge, transportation, and postdischarge orientation. Peacetime demobilizations can be undertaken in manageable phases that allow trial runs for pilot operations. Such a graduated approach enables governments and donors to improve the quality of design and implementation over time, in accordance with the lessons of experience.

A demobilization undertaken during a transition from war to peace is likely to take on the nature of an emergency relief operation. In this case it may be politically expedient to first integrate the warring factions and only later to initiate a phased demobilization, as happened in Uganda. Financial constraints may, however, preclude this option. Whichever approach is adopted, demobilization should be linked in the design stage to normal crop and school cycles, if possible. Such environmentally sensitive timing would facilitate economic and social reintegration.

Cantonment and Discharge

The cantonment of combatants in specified, easily accessible assembly areas or discharge centers (often, existing barracks) is a precondition for effective demobilization. Adequate food and health services need to be provided in the camps to avoid breakdowns in discipline and security and the outbreak of diseases. The duration of cantonment should be as short as possible: experience points to the difficulty of sustaining discipline over longer periods and to the high costs associated with this phase.

The provision of skills training or education (for example, adult literacy classes) should not be a reason for longer encampment but, at best, a result of it. Where longer cantonment cannot be avoided, implementors should ensure that the soldiers' routine includes engaging diversions such as entertainment and sports. Assembly for such activities also offers a unique opportunity to gather data for profiling and monitoring purposes.

In transitions from war to peace, disarmament takes place on surrender, in the assembly areas or in the communities. Weapons are handed over to the victorious army, to United Nations military observers, or to representatives of government institutions. In peacetime operations, soldiers are disarmed by the army before they leave the barracks for the discharge centers. It is important to ensure that soldiers in the camps are indeed disarmed and that the arms are either removed or secured in safe areas. Arms must be registered and be properly disposed of (by transferring them to an integrated national army after termination of the demobilization process, for example).

Neutral international observers can play a useful monitoring and management role in these operations. If confidence in the peace process is fragile, parties to the DRP may attempt to circumvent complete demobilization by hiding some of their forces. This practice not only contributes to the destabilization of the peace process itself but might also complicate the eventual provision of reinsertion and reintegration benefits to those combatants who are held back.

Predischarge Information and Orientation

Soldiers who have spent many years in the military are likely to lack basic knowledge about civilian life. Predischarge information and orientation sessions about what they can expect on their return to civilian life have proved beneficial. Such sessions should give ex-combatants (and, if present, their partners) information about the program in general, health issues, and civil society. In particular, ex-combatants should be briefed about their benefits and how these are to be provided and about banking and financial matters, civic and community duties, training and employment opportunities, access to land and credit, income-generating activities, and family and health issues (especially AIDS/HIV).

Female ex-combatants and female partners of ex-combatants should receive information on their legal rights, children's educational issues, family and health issues, and any special income-generation support measures available to them. Enough time should be allocated for the orientation sessions; men and women should attend specific sessions jointly; and the information should be presented in appropriate languages.

Reconciliation may also be addressed in these orientation sessions, but only if this can be done without politicizing the predischarge program. Otherwise, ex-combatants may choose not to participate in some aspects of the demobilization process, such as reporting to discharge centers. Moreover, politicizing the orientation program could endanger support from the international community.

Transportation

After discharge, ex-combatants have to be transported to their old communities or to their preferred destinations. Information about these destinations and about the numbers of spouses and dependents to be transported is crucial to the planning and execution of this complex logistical operation. Ex-combatants and their dependents might simply be given a transportation allowance, leaving travel details in their hands. Experience suggests, however, that this process should be managed centrally so that transportation prices are not inflated and the safety of ex-combatants can be ensured.

Contracts should be drawn up with either private or public transport companies to carry ex-combatants by truck, bus, or train. If available, government vehicles from the army or a ministry can be used as well. Implementors should make sure that the vehicles are roadworthy and that beneficiaries are insured during the journey. If ex-combatants will be carrying large sums in discharge payments, armed escorts should be provided.

The repatriation of ex-combatants from abroad is commonly undertaken by specialized agencies such as the United Nations High Commissioner for Refugees (UNHCR) and the International Committee of the Red Cross (ICRC). These ex-combatants may or may not be assembled in the host country for predischarge orientation. In either case, financial and logistical constraints will determine the diffusion of the ex-combatants (to regional reception centers, district capitals, or villages, for example).

Postdischarge Orientation

Many reintegration challenges confronting ex-combatants and their families are locale-specific, as geographic and cultural environments typically vary across a country. Consequently, ex-combatants and their dependents should receive orientation shortly after their arrival at their destination of choice. Counseling sessions should focus on relevant local issues such as economic opportunities, local institutions, customary rights of women, property rights, contract legalities, environmental information, and the particular social reintegration context. These sessions may also offer an opportunity to introduce the ex-combatants to local officials, community leaders, and, potentially, other ex-combatants who have been demobilized previously.

Reinsertion: The Transitional Safety Net

Once demobilized and transported to their destinations of choice, ex-combatants have to establish their lives in a civilian environment. At the same time, they may have very limited resources for sustaining themselves in the short term. Reinsertion assistance—a transitional safety net—is therefore warranted for a period of about six to twelve months (typically, one growing season). Such assistance should cover the basic needs of ex-combatants and, preferably, those of their families. Assistance should be adjusted to the cultural environment and pegged to the mode of subsistence to avoid resentment in the host communities.

Reinsertion assistance would commonly target the major survival concerns of ex-combatants and their families—food, housing, health support, and education for children (the "basic needs basket"). Cash benefits compensate ex-combatants for the loss of their income sources. Support for housing, health, and children makes up for the loss of fringe benefits that soldiers received while in service. These latter entitlements can be offered in cash or in kind, depending on three considerations: transaction costs, the financial capacity of the banking or postal system, and the logistical capacity of the implementing agency.

In the eyes of donors and NGOs, reintegration may be more attractive than other segments of the DRP because its contributions to development are more readily apparent. However, no ex-combatant can be reintegrated without having been demobilized and reinserted. Demobilization and reinsertion are thus essential to the process, and they deserve and require concerted donor support. Donor fatigue during these critical processes could inadvertently undermine the entire DRP effort.

Cash Payments

Ex-combatants need cash payments to help them meet their expenses for food, clothing, and other basic goods. Food can also be provided in kind through coupons, especially when an emergency food program is already under way. The entitlement can be calculated on the basis of indicators such as the pay received while in service, the equivalent of the poverty line, or the average income of the population in the communities of resettlement. Whatever the method of calculation, care should be taken that the cash payments do not put the ex-combatants in a privileged position with respect to the civilian community members.

Cash payments can be made in several ways. They can be paid up front—when ex-combatants leave the discharge centers, for example—or in installments. The former method is easiest to administer but has several drawbacks. Large cash injections may have an inflationary impact on the village economy, and ex-combatants may use the money "unwisely" (for instance, for purchasing alcohol or entertainment services). Moreover, carrying around large quantities of money could pose substantial security threats to ex-combatants (and to program staff).

Installment payment of cash benefits is preferable. If the cash benefits are supposed to be used for consumption purposes only, it would be advisable to make monthly or bimonthly payments. If cash benefits are also to be used for investment purposes, payment in two or three large installments might be better. In this case, the amounts should be large enough to pay for equipment or to use as collateral for loans.

Monthly payments may be small enough to be made in cash by the district office without raising security concerns. The use of bank accounts seems particularly appropriate when large payments are made in two or three installments. (The first installment, however, might be paid in cash upon departure from the discharge center or at some other specified time.) If the installment option is chosen, the capacity of the banking system, especially in rural areas, needs to be determined beforehand, and deposit and withdrawal procedures must be clearly defined.

The transaction costs incurred by the participating banks have to be included in overall program costs as a matter of course. Making payments through banks has the added benefit of educating ex-combatants about formal financial intermediation, which may eventually contribute to rural capital formation and thus to the development of the rural banking system.

Housing Assistance

Ex-combatants who did not serve for a long period may be able to return to their own homes, but usually, finding shelter is the most immediate concern of ex-combatants after their discharge. They often find temporary accommodation with relatives and friends, but such lodgings—especially in rural areas—are likely to be crowded and may increase social stress. Many ex-combatants therefore have to find temporary shelter by renting.

Housing assistance can take two different forms. Ex-combatants may receive a rent subsidy for six to twelve months, with the amount based on the size of the average ex-combatant family. One drawback of this arrangement is its potential to drive up rent in the communities. Alternatively, housing support could help pay for materials and labor for building a simple structure that the family would then own. In the former case, the subsidies would be short term and could be paid either up front or in monthly installments. In the latter case, assistance would have a lasting effect and could be provided in cash, in kind, or both ways.

In-kind materials, such as roofing sheets, are more likely than cash to be used for the intended purpose. Nevertheless, some ex-combatants might sell the in-kind contributions because they do not need them or because they need cash, especially if other inputs are delivered late. Support in the form of cash may therefore be preferable; furthermore, its transaction costs are lower, and ex-combatants can acquire the goods they need when they need them. Cash assistance could, however, create a short-term demand for a small number of goods. If this happens, the price effects on the local economy would have to be carefully considered.

Health Support

A DRP may include the provision of health services for a short time, especially if soldiers—and their families—received free health services from the army. Such assistance may be given in cash (thus effectively becoming part of the cash payment), or it could be provided through vouchers or special programs. For example, ex-combatants and their families in disease-prone areas—such as a malarial environment—could receive a voucher or money to exchange for the necessary medication.

Communities may justifiably be worried about the return of ex-combatants infected with HIV. Minimal medical screening may be undertaken during discharge, but cost considerations preclude the testing of all demobilized combatants in most instances. It would also be more appropriate to strengthen existing programs that benefit the communities at large rather than launch a new initiative. In general, the delivery of health services within a DRP should be through established government channels. The responsibility for the allocation of funds could be decentralized to enable district-based staff to respond more effectively to the needs of a particular environment.

Education Support for Children

Ex-combatants who suffer a loss of income may decide to curtail expenses for their children's education, especially that of girls. A program component targeting children may relieve ex-combatants from a short-term cash shortage and enable children to continue schooling for at least one school year. Such support could encompass the provision of fees, uniforms, books, and other materials. Education assistance should be provided through vouchers that can be reimbursed at the schools (and shops) of choice rather than in cash.

Education support, including materials, should be implemented in close cooperation with and through the public education system, especially at the local level. All biological children of ex-combatants—as well as orphans in the care of ex-combatants, in hardship cases—of primary and secondary school age should be eligible for this support; their number can be established with the help of the monitoring system. Again, decentralized allocation of funds, on the basis of the number of ex-combatants in each district, seems appropriate because schools (especially in rural areas) and program staff must necessarily be in close contact with each other.

Reintegration: The Ultimate Objective

For ex-combatants, families, and communities alike, reintegration is a continuous, long-term process that takes place on social, political, and economic levels. Social and political reintegration is broadly defined as the acceptance of an ex-combatant and his or her family by the host community and its leaders. Economic reintegration implies the financial independence of an ex-combatant's household through productive and gainful employment.

Long-term reintegration ultimately is the yardstick by which the success of a DRP is measured. Successful long-term reintegration can make a major contribution to national conflict resolution and to the restoration of social capital. Conversely, failure to achieve reintegration can lead to considerable insecurity at the societal and individual levels, including rent-seeking behavior through the barrel of a gun.

Reintegration assistance measures should be prioritized according to their degree of complexity—with the simplest steps being implemented first—to facilitate early confidence building and rapid implementation. Speed of implementation should be an important criterion for any reintegration measure because ex-combatants are most vulnerable in the first two years after demobilization. It is advisable both to use existing government and NGO manpower, technical resources, and infrastructure and to avoid duplication of existing structures and programs.

The components of a reintegration program should be complementary and should be linked conceptually and in practice. All reintegration support should be provided for a limited time only, however, to avoid creating dependence. Moreover, DRPs should not attempt to reform entire sectors of an economy. On the contrary, linking the DRP to normal development programs (by restructuring existing portfolios or through targeting ongoing programs) is desirable.

Information, Counseling, and Referral

Ex-combatants commonly lack information about the economic opportunities available to them on their return to civilian life. An information, counseling, and referral service can assist ex-combatants in crucial ways. First, it can provide answers to questions about access to reintegration entitlements and other more general issues; counseling on job-seeking strategies; information and counseling on training, employment, and credit opportunities; and advice on microproject identification and design. Second, it offers a means for linking ex-combatants to such opportunities. This kind of service can play a key role in integrating the education, training, employment, and credit components of a reintegration support program, and it can provide valuable monitoring information. Finally, it can provide critical social-psychological support during this difficult transition period.

Rural Strategy

Resettlement is not synonymous with reintegration. Access to arable land and to supportive social capital is the main determinant of successful rural reintegration. Any strategy for sustainable rural reintegration must identify suitable areas for resettlement and ensure that ex-combatants have clear title or secure rights to the land, either individually or as part of a resettlement program.

It may be preferable to locate ex-combatants in their communities of origin or where they have relatives (and hence an existing social support system), rather than to try to build social capital among strangers in a new area. If the latter approach must be chosen, the beneficiaries and members of surrounding communities must be involved throughout the process of economic and social reintegration for it to be successful.

Additional components of rural reintegration include the rehabilitation of basic infrastructure (such as water, health, and school facilities) through quick impact projects and the provision of appropriate seeds, tools, fertilizers, and draft animals. The needs of different occupations—those of sedentary agriculturists and pastoralists, for example—should be taken into account. Providing information about and access to ongoing rural credit schemes may also be useful.

Urban Strategy

Given the relative complexity of urban labor markets, support measures for urban reintegration generally need to be more diverse and of longer duration than those for rural reintegration. Creation of public sector employment can be effective for preventing unemployment in the short run. This may include public works schemes, limited absorption into the civil service (including the civilian police force), and hiring into specialized services (the health field, for example). Special labor-intensive public works may provide immediate employment opportunities for many unskilled ex-combatants.

However, these are short-term interventions that are costly to sustain. The preferable course would be to expand ongoing public works programs to cover ex-combatants. Large-scale absorption of ex-combatants into the civil service ought to be avoided because such employment could foster ex-combatants' dependence on the government and could have deleterious budgetary implications.

Ex-combatants who acquired marketable skills in the military can better compete in the labor market if their skills can be verified. Skills certification is the least expensive intervention and could have a beneficial impact. It should be done by the appropriate line ministry or civilian agency to ensure credibility in the private sector. Ex-combatants who wish to complete their primary or secondary education should be given the financial means to do so and provided with necessary technical assistance, such as help with applications.

Vocational training can provide ex-combatants with marketable skills. DRP implementors should refrain from duplicating existing facilities or establishing elaborate independent programs and infrastructure. Instead, they should contract existing training suppliers to enhance provision and should make sure that ex-combatants have the financial means (in the form of vouchers, for example) to attend the training institutions of their choice. Such training can be geared to the skills and needs of the ex-combatants.

This approach would ensure that training is demand driven, enhances consumer choice, and improves local capacity. Vocational training in itself is not enough, however, to ensure employment or economic reintegration. It should be linked to employment referral or self-employment schemes. Tool kits can also be furnished to ex-combatant trainees or graduates to enable them to start a business or to enhance their value to potential employers. Particular emphasis must be placed on the timely availability of these tools.

Job-creation programs supplying temporary wage subsidies or tax credits to employers, or a combination of the two, can be an important component after training. These programs would help ex-combatants gain practical experience with a private employer for six months to a year. Such on-the-job training would also enhance ex-combatants' longer-term employment opportunities by providing job networking and skills acquisition simultaneously.

A major prerequisite for such programs is cooperation with the private sector, which the government should begin promoting early in the design process. Apprenticeship in the informal sector combines the benefits of vocational training and employment subsidies at the lower end of the market and is thus a feasible and cost-effective option for most urban ex-combatants.

Microenterprise credit schemes can help ex-combatants secure their economic independence and self-employment. Experience suggests that such schemes need to be accompanied by rudimentary business training and counseling for the beneficiaries, however, and by significant micromanagement on the part of project staff. Whether such schemes should offer concessional credit rates depends on whether DRP designers feel that socioeconomic and political considerations outweigh purely economic concerns. In general, such schemes are the most expensive interventions and the most difficult to manage.

Special Target Groups

Female ex-combatants often find it more difficult than male ex-combatants to achieve economic reintegration. Special measures may have to be instituted to ensure that female beneficiaries have equal training and employment opportunities. For example, funding for child care and provision of training to women in their areas of professional interest and in the villages where they reside should be considered. Women and child ex-soldiers may also receive preferential access to specific program components through affirmative action. Efforts should be made to ensure that child soldiers are reunited with their families (or are placed in foster care), have access to education, and receive psychosocial counseling.

Disabled ex-combatants commonly require tailored training and employment assistance. They should have access to this specialized training (often in medical rehabilitation institutions) and to capital, which would enable them to ensure their financial independence through participation in microprojects and employment support programs. In addition, the special needs of severely disabled and chronically ill ex-combatants should be met through institutionalized care.

Soldiers who are close to retirement may be another primary target group for demobilization. The general terms and conditions of service should be applicable in these cases, and the government's pension scheme should cover soldiers demobilized on the grounds of age. Direct reintegration support may be extended as well, but it should be limited to hardship cases. A similar approach should apply to soldiers serving under special contracts that are based on a gratuity scheme.

Reintegration and Poverty

Demobilization and reintegration programs can be justified on two grounds: they help defuse social tension, and they assist a particularly vulnerable group in building a new life. However, reintegration is a long and complex process without a clear conclusion; even comprehensive programs in a favorable macroeconomic environment cannot by themselves ensure that the living standards of ex-combatants will equal those of the poorer segments of the civilian population.

In Uganda, for example, the annual income of ex-combatants during the reintegration phase of the DRP was estimated at less than half the already low national average for the working population, despite a coherent policy framework. The success of a DRP must sometimes be judged by whether strife is avoided, the basic needs of the most vulnerable are met, and conditions for long-term progress are improved: outright eradication of poverty among ex-combatants may not always be possible.

Beyond Reintegration

Many ex-combatants, especially the disabled, pensioners, and women heading households, may need assistance beyond the completion date of the DRP. It is therefore important that DRP support be designed so that it can easily be incorporated into ongoing or future government development efforts. Consequently, government funds (as well as donor and NGO funds) will have to be made available over the long run for ex-combatants, even when they are no longer a separate target group.

Support for the reintegration of ex-combatants (and for internally displaced persons and returning refugees) may have to be complemented by investments in economic and social infrastructure, especially when population densities in communities increase significantly. Hence, to achieve maximum impact, a DRP has to be anchored in a coherent, long-term program for reconstruction and development.

2

The Social and Institutional Context

This chapter discusses the wider social and institutional aspects of re-integration. *Social dimensions* reflect an often neglected but neverthe-less important consideration for successful reintegration: the effects of stigmatization and the acceptance or rejection of ex-combatants by host communities. *Institutional and management* issues cut across the three seamless phases by setting the framework for the implementation process and improving its functioning. Finally, *external assistance* has a fundamental and complementary role in program implementation.

Social Dimensions: Rebuilding Social Capital

Combatants, particularly those who were recruited by force or who served for many years, may welcome the opportunity to leave the military legally. By and large, they will be mentally prepared to face the challenge of reintegration. Specific subgroups, however, may face more profound problems with social reintegration. For example, social reintegration is often difficult for female ex-combatants, who are likely to have become accustomed to an independent and egalitarian way of life in the military; they understandably find it hard to adapt to the expectations of traditional communities.

Female partners of ex-combatants who migrate to communities with different ethnic, linguistic, or cultural backgrounds are often initially rejected. They are particularly vulnerable if their spouses abandon them, become incapacitated, or die. An array of special measures for promoting the social reintegration of women can be put in place: community support groups can be created, women can be provided information on their legal rights, and communities can be sensitized to women's needs and rights.

Many military forces recruit children, especially during wartime. There is little experience with measures in support of this extremely vulnerable group, but common sense suggests that child soldiers should receive psychosocial counseling, access to education and health services, and help in reuniting them with their families or with placing them in foster care. In war-to-peace operations, it may be advisable to reintegrate them with displaced and refugee children rather than with adult ex-combatants. Communities should be sensitized to the particular needs and abilities of this group.

For ex-combatants, the programming part of economic and social-psychological reintegration is just one side of the equation. Often overlooked, but equally important, are the attitudes and capacities of the receiving community. The community side of the equation might be viewed as the social capital that must incorporate the human capital of the individual soldier. Just how well can a war-devastated social infrastructure receive and support ex-combatants?

Two social factors have emerged as particularly critical to the reintegration process. First is the negative label or stigma that an ex-combatant sometimes carries. In peacetime, there may be a generalized fear that ex-combatants are illiterate thugs, conveyers of violence, crime, and sexually transmitted diseases. This fear is amplified when ex-combatants are demobilized because they are deemed to be chronically ill (with AIDS/HIV infection, for example) or unfit for the military, perhaps because of alcoholism or lack of discipline. When communities reject ex-combatants, community fears and expectations may well become a self-fulfilling prophecy. Therefore, stigmatizing labels must be avoided during implementation or promptly combated when they appear.

The second critical dimension concerns the degree of social cohesiveness, trust, and organizational density—that is, the social capital—in the receiving community. The social capital can be a support network for the ex-combatant, providing information, a sympathetic ear, credit, and access to other productive assets. Ex-combatants should be encouraged to strengthen their social networks by, for example, attending religious ceremonies and participating in sports events or community groups.

Several approaches might help prepare the community and reduce the stigma that may be attached to ex-combatants. For example, district administrators and community leaders can be trained and charged with sensitizing the community through meetings with community members. Radio broadcasts in local languages and popular folk media (for instance, theater groups) can further mutual understanding of the reintegration process. Religious support groups (such as church- or mosque-based committees) can play also a key role in supporting reintegration. Finally, psychosocial counseling by specially trained staff may be offered to ex-combatants and community members alike.

Communication and sensitization activities conducted before ex-combatants are discharged should stress that most ex-soldiers are returning as family units and that the benefit package they bring with them will not only sustain them through a harvest season but could also contribute to the village economy. Care should be taken, however, that community members are not led to make overly optimistic assumptions about the ex-combatants' financial ability (to aid extended families, for example).

A program that provides visible benefits to host communities is much likelier to be successful than one that benefits only the ex-combatants. In addition, experience shows that social reintegration is often eased by the support of an extended family network, and ex-combatants might well be encouraged to reintegrate in the vicinity of their extended families. Finally, communities that mobilized their children for service in the army should be educated about their responsibilities for receiving and assisting them as demobilized ex-combatants.

In the absence of dense social capital in the receiving communities, ex-combatants often form self-help support groups on their return. These groups, as well as mixed groups of ex-combatants and other community members, can help alleviate initial community mistrust and alienation among ex-combatants. Program interventions should support formation of such groups. The restoration of social capital, the use of family networks, and the provision of mutual help among ex-combatants all help prevent ex-combatants from resorting to crime.

In general, the sensitivity of communities toward reconciliation is greater in transitions from war to peace, but it is in this situation that the social capital is usually the most devastated. For a reintegration program to be fully effective, then, a critical step is to understand the local sociocultural context that ex-combatants will encounter when they return: the ethnic mix, the traditional land tenure patterns, and the organizational density (which affects the community's ability to support and nurture its returning sons and daughters). Rapid ethnographic assessments of social capital are the method of choice.

Institutional Concerns: The Key

Implementation of a DRP should be the responsibility of a single specialized civilian institution. Even when that body must be established quickly, its structure should be well planned. Preferably, such an institution should be outside the regular government structure but linked to it by a board or advisory committee. The board's responsibility is best limited to overall guidance and political backing. As a political body, the board should avoid involvement in day-to-day management.

Although dissolving this single-purpose implementation agency after the program is completed eliminates one layer of bureaucracy, some minimal services—information, regulation, and advocacy—will still need to be provided. The government can integrate outstanding activities into its mainstream development efforts, and other ongoing needs can be met through a combination of government offices, NGOs, and community-supported local organizations.

DRPs comprise two distinct types of interventions: short-term safety nets (possibly during an emergency situation) and longer-term development efforts. If a single institution is in charge of all DRP activities, its structure has to be flexible enough to accommodate their diverse tasks. If other institutions or organizations (government agencies, donors, or

NGOs) are involved in a DRP, the lead institution should have the clear and generally accepted mandate of coordination so that overlaps in coverage can be avoided in the program design. Existing specialized institutions may be the best vehicles for implementing certain program components (for instance, the provision of health services).

The administrative costs of a commission (including field offices) may be high. The lower the transaction costs, the larger the amounts available to ex-combatants and the greater the donors' interest in the program. Particular attention should therefore be paid to administrative costs in relation to overall program costs. Total transaction costs of approximately 10 percent are tolerable. The administrative costs of the demobilization phase of a transition from war to peace may run higher, however, because of the need for elaborate logistical systems.

Field Representation and Decentralization

A DRP can have implications for practically every part of a country. Decentralization of decisionmaking authority during program implementation enhances flexibility and responsiveness to local conditions and needs. Community offices at the provincial or district level bring the program closest to its beneficiaries, and they should be established on the basis of the distribution of ex-combatants across regions. They can be staffed in part with officials from the local administration to ensure that the DRP is linked to overall development activities. For such an arrangement to be successful, the local administration has to be actively involved.

To maximize a program's relevance, community offices ought to have a fair amount of autonomy regarding decisionmaking and funds allocation, and community-based staff should have the mobility to reach the ex-combatants in their constituency. Headquarters could be limited to a supporting role, provided that accountability does not suffer, especially when implementation is complex. This arrangement requires a great deal of coordination between the central and local levels. Frequent, regular visits by headquarters staff to the districts or provinces and regular (perhaps quarterly) meetings of all staff are particularly beneficial.

Community and Beneficiary Involvement

The best strategy for overcoming community resentment is to actively involve community members in the implementation process. This may be done by including community representatives—say, traditional leaders or elected members—in local committees with decisionmaking authority. For example, they can be made responsible for the distribution of tools and seeds and for the organization of labor. Local committees should be consulted regularly by program staff.

It can also be useful to include officials of all relevant local administration offices in a committee at the provincial or district level. If nothing else, such committees may prevent administrators from obstructing the DRP. Formal links to the local administration should ensure the incorporation of a DRP as a local multisectoral intervention into the regular work program of local officials—in particular, in education, health, and agriculture.

On account of their motivation and their familiarity with reintegration problems, representatives of ex-combatants can play an important role in program execution. Ex-combatants should be encouraged to elect their representatives—say, once every two years. These representatives can interact horizontally with other ex-combatants for problem solving and vertically with community-based program staff. It is advisable to reimburse these representatives for the expenses they incur while performing their duties, especially for travel and per diem.

The Role of Nongovernmental Organizations

NGOs can serve as effective intermediaries between the government, donors, and beneficiaries in the implementation of a DRP. They often play a prominent role in humanitarian relief efforts and have a grass-roots understanding of the communities within which they work. They are thus in a unique position to help community offices translate program design into effective intervention. The challenge for many NGOs is to transform themselves from emergency agencies into development agencies with pertinent technical knowledge and to coordinate their activities with the central government.

Management Aspects: Critical Ingredients

Staffing

Appropriate staff personality, experience, and motivation are crucial for successful program implementation. Community-based staff and ex-combatant representatives (as well as community committees) are the major mediators in disputes between ex-combatants and community members. It would therefore be advisable to employ qualified ex-combatants who are trusted by male and female ex-combatants and communities alike within central and community offices.

Because the skills of project staff may not be sufficient for program administration or implementation, especially for counseling and reporting, staff training that focuses on practical problem solving should be high on the agenda. Staff training, at least at a basic level, is most useful when undertaken before demobilization. Training sessions can then be repeated during program implementation when the need arises.

Monitoring, Reporting, and Evaluation

Because the implementation of a DRP is highly decentralized, it is important for program management to have up-to-date information on the progress of operations and the ability to speedily redirect operations, if necessary. To this end, a management information system (MIS) should be installed and launched before ex-combatants are discharged. Ideally, the MIS would collect data on individual ex-combatants throughout the implementation process. Standardized questionnaires could be distributed, starting in the discharge centers and later when ex-combatants access benefits (when they receive their second cash installment, for instance).

It is the responsibility of the community-based staff to report accurately to the central office on administrative matters concerning ongoing operations. The central office is responsible for analyzing community-level information and monitoring progress. Constant and close contact between central and community offices to improve decisionmaking efficiency is thus essential for an effective MIS.

The MIS is a potent but complex management tool. It may be necessary to hire a specialist (perhaps through a donor agency) to assist management in establishing and running such a computer-based system. An MIS also calls for a good deal of training of community-based staff. If local implementation capacity proves too limited to provide detailed information on individual ex-combatants, it may be advisable to limit the MIS to monitoring the implementation of DRP components only. In both cases, clear benchmarks against which the program can be evaluated should be established.

Evaluation of a DRP after the program has been completed allows assessment of both achievements and impacts. The program's achievements can be evaluated by comparing the benchmarks with actual implementation performance. (For example, did as many ex-combatants as expected benefit from a specific component of the program?) An impact assessment would evaluate the consequences of the program for the ex-combatants, their families, and the communities of settlement.

Either qualitative or quantitative methods can be employed for the impact assessment, but the qualitative method is likely to be less expensive, and it is likely to capture the individual experiences of social and economic reintegration better. Regardless of the level and method of the analysis selected, independent consultants should undertake evaluation of the program some time after its completion, or after completion of individual program phases.

Accounting and Auditing

DRPs are usually too expensive to implement without external financial support. It is therefore important that program management follow proper accounting procedures and avoid financial irregularities so that funding is not jeopardized. Again, the employment of a specialist may be necessary to ensure quality standards. Accounting should be accompanied by regular auditing, either monthly or quarterly, by an independent consultant, possibly an international auditing firm. Accounting and auditing to ensure proper use of funds can build trust between donors and the government.

External Assistance: Help and Hindrance

Donors and NGOs are vital contributors to DRPs—the former mainly for funding purposes, the latter more for implementation. The role of donor governments, however, needs to be understood in a broader context. Often, it was external sources that provided the means of destruction in the first place. Between 1985 and 1994 about $12 billion (in constant 1990 prices) worth of arms was exported to Sub-Saharan Africa.[1] By contrast, the Ethiopian DRP for 475,000 ex-combatants—the largest thus far in Africa—cost around $195 million. Although external arms sales have been decreasing, money spent for arms still dwarfs that for DRPs.

Strategies and Timing

A number of donors and NGOs specialize in assistance for demobilization (relief), reinsertion, or reintegration (development). Emergency relief agencies, especially the UNHCR and the ICRC, have clear strategies and have repeatedly provided timely and crucial support to demobilization and reinsertion phases on humanitarian assistance grounds. Donors' development agencies, by contrast, have generally

---

1. Dollar amounts are current U.S. dollars. A billion is a thousand million.

lacked the ability to respond quickly. Even when they had pledged financial support to a DRP early in the process, they often made resources available only after considerable delay. In fact, the World Bank's statutes have precluded activity in many countries experiencing prolonged conflicts because of those countries' nonaccrual status or the failure of the state apparatus.

Part of the reason for these delays is that donors' disbursement procedures have not yet been adapted to the nature of a DRP, whether it takes place during peacetime or during a transition from war to peace. In particular, donors' budgetary cycles have seldom been synchronized with the schedules for program implementation. Beyond such structural problems, most donors have to resolve legal issues that arise when support to former combatants, an army, or a ministry of defense is contemplated. Furthermore, most donors have not yet adopted a strategy toward DRPs that clearly acknowledges the status of demobilization as a development issue, not simply a political and military matter.

Donors need to realize the extent to which they can help or hinder the design and implementation of DRPs. Without a comprehensive, targeted strategy and accompanying changes in their operating practices, donors are likely to continue to send contradictory signals to governments about the extent and purpose of their support. They would thus continue to be seen as unreliable partners who might renege on pledges, shift priorities during implementation, or fail to see the connection between emergency relief and development.

Differing Agenda

Donors and NGOs have shown a tendency to impose their own interests in determining what assistance to provide and how, rather than to adapt their support to the needs of the country. For instance, some donors have attached political conditions to aid, and some have initiated DRP activities that parallel other such efforts without much consultation with the government. As a result, materials were procured that were not suitable for the environment (one example is vehicles) or were expensive to deliver (such as roofing sheets).

Some NGOs may also be inclined to provide support on the basis of ethnicity or religion. In all these cases, tensions may arise between the government, donors, and NGOs that can easily derail even a well-planned program. Support (especially technical assistance) provided by donors to specific preferred components of a program should be cost-effective and part of a comprehensive program.

Coordination

Coordination has to take place on two levels: between the government and donors, including NGOs, and within the donor and NGO community. For each level and each phase, transparent mechanisms for coordination should be developed and adhered to. Coordination between donors and NGOs is essential for constructing a comprehensive response to a government program. Without a lead agency (not necessarily the major donor) to coordinate activities and financial support, valuable synergy effects are generally forgone, and administrative requirements are multiplied.

Especially in postconflict situations, government capacity at the central and local levels is generally weak regarding both program design and implementation. In such cases (for example, in Mozambique), multilateral and bilateral donors may be tempted to assume the government's functions in order to commence operations rapidly. Such an approach, however, does not automatically ensure either the coordination of donor interests or speed in implementation. It may also alienate the government, especially when capacity-building measures have not been included, and it could threaten the long-term sustainability of the program after donors withdraw or change their focus.

The most effective approach seems to be joint development of a DRP in a partnership of the government, on the one side, and donors and NGOs, led by one agency, on the other. In this case, as in Uganda, ownership will be strong on both sides, and disagreements about design and implementation can be dealt with at the technical rather than the political level.

3
Early Warning Signals and Preventive Actions

The discussion so far has focused on best practices for designing and implementing a DRP. However, there is much to be learned from the things that have gone wrong, to varying degrees, in all of the programs to date. DRPS, of course, share the implementation difficulties of any project or program interventions. But because of the nature and objectives of DRPS, the implications of such difficulties are far-reaching: unresolved problems can have negative consequences for overall security and peace in a country. Angola's first attempt at demobilization is a disconcerting example of how program failure can increase the risks to a country's stability.

Although the DRP concept developed in the preceding chapters can be applied rather universally, country conditions always vary. Just as the program design has to reflect specific political, social, and economic characteristics, so any DRP will face a wide spectrum of specific design and implementation problems that cannot all be anticipated. However, there are also problem areas common to a number of countries or situations. Once these issues are identified in a given context, experience can be used to improve on DRP design and implementation in other countries.

Table 3.1, drawing on a synthesis of experience to date, presents early warning signals that may have a severe negative impact on program implementation, as well as examples of potential negative consequences in a variety of contexts and possible preventive actions. The examples and responses are meant as suggestions: the list is not exhaustive, and the possible consequences and preventive actions listed may not be applicable in all circumstances.

Table 3.1 Warning Signals and Preventive Actions for Ensuring Effective DRPs

Early warning signal	Possible consequence	Preventive action
Political dimensions		
Neglect of DRP issues during peace negotiations.	Transfer of responsibilities to inexperienced government; late program development; underfunding of DRP activities.	Recognize issue and include relevant provisions in peace accord.
Lack of commitment and leadership of warring factions.	Political interference during implementation; change of course midway; lack of support when problems cannot be solved at the program level; resumption of armed conflict.	Convince all parties involved that a DRP is in the utmost interest of the country; involve all warring factions in program design; link aid to peaceful transition.
Ethnic or regional discrimination; incomplete national reconciliation.	Creation of resentment among ethnic groups; resumption of hostile activities.	Depoliticize the program; base differences in benefits on neutral indicators only (mode of subsistence, health, gender, rank, age).
Political pressure for short-term intervention and piecemeal planning.	Incomplete design; component overlaps; postponement of sustainable solution; inefficiencies in implementation.	Agree on comprehensive approach with complete design before implementation; do not trade quality of preparations for speed in starting implementation; explore and clearly present strategic and operational options.

Table 3.1   (*continued*)

Early warning signal	Possible consequence	Preventive action
	Targeting	
Incomplete identification of ex-combatants (keeping an army in reserve, unwilling-ness of ex-combatants to report, ad hoc approach).	Incomplete coverage of future beneficiaries; demonstrations of those initially left out; need for program redesign if funds are limited; loss of government's credibility among ex-combatants.	Alert policymakers and military leaders to long-term consequences of holding back troops; encourage mutual trust; encourage government to build trust towards ex-combatants (policy of "no retaliation"); plan identification process ahead of time.
Program targeted to ex-combatants only.	Needs of spouses and children remain unat-tended; poverty deep-ened.	Design program compo-nents around the ex-combatant family rather than the individual, wherever possible; identify their needs and numbers beforehand.
Failure to consult communities in the design process.	Inability to secure donor financial support.	Ensure community participation.
Failure to conduct studies of socioeconomic profiles and land and labor markets.	Failed social and economic reintegration; inappropriate assistance for reinsertion and reintegration.	Make preparatory studies on needs and conditions a priority.

Early warning signal	Possible consequence	Preventive action
	Demobilization	
Incomplete disarmament.	Resumption of hostilities easier if peace process fails; armed criminal activities on the part of discontented ex-combatants.	In assembly areas, ensure that weapons are removed from the centers and securely stored; link access to entitlements to relinquishment of weapons (arms receipts).
Prolonged encampment in assembly areas.	Breakdown in discipline and motivation; rioting and demonstrations; kidnapping of project staff; regional insecurity; difficulty in providing basic services; substantial costs.	Locate camps where easily serviceable (especially food, water, health); ensure that funding and logistics are in place before encampment; ensure duration does not exceed time necessary for registration, data collection, and predischarge orientation.
Politicization of predischarge orientation.	Ethnically-based hostilities may continue; failure of national reconciliation; creation of overly optimistic expectations about civilian life; ex- combatant discontent and unrest.	Focus orientation on civic, social, economic, and program issues; avoid promises that program implementors cannot keep.
	Reinsertion	
Reinsertion package substantially higher than average income.	Resentment on the part of communities and other vulnerable groups; rejection of ex-combatants on their return; creation of dependency syndrome.	Calculate package on the basis of basic needs for no more than one year; incorporate expenses for family health care and educational support for children.
Delays in delivery of in-kind entitlements.	Support may be inappropriate or useless when finally rendered; delay-induced cash expenses for ex-combatants.	Initiate planning early, especially for logistical requirements; consider monetizing benefits.

Table 3.1   *(continued)*

Early warning signal	Possible consequence	Preventive action
Reintegration		
Shortage of arable land; high population density.	Failed rural reintegration; criminal activities; unrest; extended and costly assistance requirements beyond the DRP.	Initiate or reorient political process regarding land tenure before implementation; avoid singling out ex-combatants; undertake study on land opportunity structure.
Construction of special facilities, (for example, vocational training centers).	High construction and transaction costs; long start-up period; difficulty of transferring into regular structure on termination.	Use existing facilities; speedy implementation of a high-quality program is crucial; if special facilities have to be constructed, ensure beforehand that responsible ministry is included in its design and operation from the outset.
Provision of training while in service.	Comparative disadvantage vis-à-vis specialized institutions; lack of qualified staff; high cost of longer army service or encampment; supply-driven training.	Empower the beneficiaries to select the training of their choice (demand-driven approach); establish inventory, capacity, and willingness to cooperate of existing training institutions beforehand.
Large-scale absorption of ex-combatants in public service and parastatals.	Net effect on government expenditures reduced; shifting of longer-term financial solution to other ministries.	Encourage the private sector to hire and train ex-combatants; devise strategy for comprehensive employment support.
Design of a multisectoral DRP as an independent program intervention.	Overlaps with existing programs in the areas of concern; duplication of effort; waste of resources; skepticism and unwillingness to support on the part of other ministries.	Enhance synergy and reduce implementation burden by linking to ongoing efforts; solicit support from government agencies and other implementors and encourage their participation in implementation; incorporate any longer-term activities into regular development efforts after termination of the DRP.
Program support without specific termination date.	Creation of dependency syndrome; long-term drain on resources; community resentment.	Devise specific time frame for support; cover any needs thereafter under ongoing programs.

Early warning signal	Possible consequence	Preventive action
Social dimensions		
Extensive support to ex-combatants only.	Creation of a privileged group; community resentment; expensive when extended to other groups.	Extend coverage of ongoing activities instead of creating new ones, wherever possible; closely coordinate activities; include community support activities.
Neglect of the fears and needs of the communities.	Community resentment; hesitance to welcome ex-combatants; high social costs of reintegration.	Encourage community participation in design and implementation; regularly consult communities; ensure proper publicity for program.
Negative labeling (stigmatization) of ex-combatants.	Self-fulfilling prophecy; rejection of ex-combatants by receiving communities without justification.	Undertake continuous community awareness activities before program implementation; regularly assess the status of social reintegration.
Institutional and management issues		
Planning of DRP activities by various agencies independently.	Lack of coordination; overlaps and possible gaps in coverage; waste of resources.	Integrate all activities under a single civilian body for coordination (and implementation); ensure that activities are complementary and mutually reinforcing.
Centralized decisionmaking structure.	Lack of motivation of local program staff; central decisions may not be appropriate for a local environment; loss of central government authority.	Ensure flexibility and responsiveness to local needs; involve local program staff, communities, and beneficiaries in decisionmaking.
Lack of professional accounting and auditing procedures.	Misuse of funds; unnecessarily high transaction costs; ex-combatant discontent; loss of donor confidence.	Install a professional accounting system; provide for regular external auditing; ensure transparent handling of funds.

Table 3.1   (*continued*)

Early warning signal	Possible consequence	Preventive action
	External assistance	
Lack of strategy and coordination of efforts.	Delayed response to government request; duplication of programs; inefficiency; competition.	Have donors and government agree on one lead agency for donor coordination and guidance; persuade donors to join program rather than devise separate initiatives; present strategic and operational options; include NGOs.
Refusal of, or delays in, honoring pledges.	Derailment of the program; implementation may have to be suspended; loss of government trust.	Ensure timely replenishment of funds; enable donors to anticipate funding requests by involving them in a transparent manner; recommend that donors adjust their disbursement procedures, if necessary.
Particular interests and tied aid.	Government resentment; unjustified adjustments to the program; costly or inappropriate support.	Develop program jointly with government, donors, and NGOs; resolve disputes on a technical level; accept tied aid when it blends well with the program.
Donors and NGOs proceed without government counterpart.	Government resentment; risk to long-term sustainability; creation of a "parallel government."	Build capacities throughout the process; urge government to identify counterpart with decisionmaking authority; convince donors to adjust speed rather than bypass government.

4
The Economic Impact: Assessing the Peace Dividend

War inflicts human and material losses on the society and the economy. Quantifying the loss to people is practically impossible: the suffering, pain, and traumatization caused by war cannot be measured. Calculating the economic losses attributable to war is a simpler proposition.

The economic benefits of ending a war extend well beyond savings in military-related costs. A DRP affects the economy on both macroeconomic and microeconomic levels. On the one hand, it contributes to a restructuring of government spending; on the other, many people enter the civilian labor market. Both effects should ultimately lead to economic growth, and they can be analyzed by identifying financial and economic returns.

Analyzing the peace dividend for one country may not provide a great deal of information. When compared with the economic effects in other countries undergoing a DRP, however, that information becomes a valuable tool for understanding the challenges of postwar reconstruction and evaluating the success of a program. Nevertheless, economic losses and returns need to be interpreted in the specific social, political, and economic context of a country. (Chapter 5 summarizes indicators for the peace dividend in Ethiopia, Namibia, and Uganda; see table 5.3.)

The Costs of War

In assessing the costs of war to an economy, one would ideally calculate the destruction of the production factors (labor, capital, and knowledge) to determine the country's potential output without war and then compare this information with the actual output. However, making these ideal computations is difficult, time-consuming, and beyond the scope of this study. In the absence of data on estimated potential output, the comparison of growth rates of gross domestic product (GDP) at factor cost or of basic prices before, during, and after the war may serve as an approximation. Depending on a country's economic structure, this analysis can be refined further by disaggregating GDP into agriculture (subsistence and commercial); other primary industries, such as mining and fishing; secondary industries, especially manufacturing; and tertiary industries (in particular, trade and transport).

Even these calculations entail various methodological problems and are inherently difficult to undertake. Countries at war normally place little emphasis on the regular collection of data, and it is therefore unlikely that adequate time-series data exist for compiling meaningful averages. For instance, civil war in Ethiopia began in the early 1960s; reliable data for the prewar period and for most of the war period are not available.

Moreover, the data that do get collected are usually incomplete. This situation is compounded by the continuing weakness of central statistical offices in many African countries. Consequently, only the economic losses incurred in the last years of war may be calculable with some accuracy, with data consolidated by the postwar government.

It is often difficult to distinguish the impact of war from other macroeconomic effects. In Ethiopia the drought of 1984–85 led to a decrease of GDP at factor cost of almost 10 percent in real terms. Even while the war was going on, growth caught up and reached almost 14 percent two years later. Obviously, then, war is not necessarily synonymous with low or negative growth rates.

There is yet another reason why it may not be feasible to isolate the economic effects of war. The intensity of war may change over time, as may the economic activities of the population, which are based on experience and expectations. For example, low-intensity warfare, especially when regionally limited, may lead to relatively modest losses, as in Namibia. There, GDP growth surpassed the average for lower-middle-income countries even during the final years of war. The current conflict in northern Sri Lanka is another case in point.

In fact, authoritarian forms of government (for example, a military dictatorship) may engender higher economic losses than low-intensity warfare does, through general insecurity caused by expropriation, expulsion, and the unpredictability of political action. The economic loss resulting from such government actions can indeed be substantial, as in Uganda in the 1970s.

Evidence from the case studies reveals that peace does not bring immediate economic recovery. It may take one or more years for the population to regain trust and for growth to resume. Thereafter, growth rates for the first few years, starting from a much reduced base, are commonly impressive but not necessarily sustainable. (Ethiopia is one example.) Calculating the potential output on the basis of postwar growth may therefore lead to an overestimate of losses.

Consequently, other growth rates may have to serve as counterfactuals: for example, the average long-term growth rate of the country (during and after war) may be contrasted to the average long-term growth rate of the entire region (Sub-Saharan Africa). Once the economic cost of war has been established, it can be compared with, for example, the actual GDP at factor cost, the government's defense expenditures during war, or the costs of a DRP.

Financial Returns

Whatever the cause for demobilization, the financial returns are reflected in the potential reduction of a government's military spending in favor of peaceful and productive uses, notably in social sectors. As the numbers of soldiers decline, so too do recurrent expenditures on defense. In a transition from war to peace, the potential for reducing capital expenditures is evident. The financial returns from both sources can be substantial. Their calculation on the basis of government finance data, however, is not necessarily straightforward for at least three reasons: off-budget expenses, lack of budget comparability in different periods, and budgetary flexibility.

Civil wars are fought by at least two armies, only one of which is covered under the government budget. Expenses incurred by guerrilla forces are commonly unknown, as are their sources of funding. In such circumstances, the calculated financial returns to peace (including demobilization) will always underestimate the real financial returns. When armies from other countries are involved in the war, the underestimation is even greater, and establishing those expenditures for the war may be impossible. Furthermore, military spending may be stated incorrectly in the budget from the outset (illegal arms imports to bypass United Nations sanctions, for example).

A war of independence may result in the creation of new states or governments. Military spending before peace is budgeted by one country (excepting support from other countries that goes to liberation fighters), but spending after peace shows up in the budgets of two or more countries. Gaining access to all these different sources may be as difficult a task as consolidating the data that have been gathered.

Restructuring of expenditures might not free up resources for other uses even when all military expenses are accurately budgeted. In peacetime, in particular, a government may be forced to demobilize because it cannot continue to fund its army; the savings would then be used to reduce the deficit. Furthermore, part of the savings may be used by the government to improve the quality of military services. Finally, the DRP may be budgeted under the ministry of defense and thus reduce the savings in the short term. It should also be borne in mind that a restructuring in favor of social expenditures does not support the poor unless these expenditures are clearly targeted and effectively implemented.

Despite such limitations, the calculation of financial returns can offer helpful insights about the usefulness of the program from a macroeconomic perspective. Several indicators capture these effects well: the ratio of defense spending to overall government spending (if figures are available for recurrent and capital expenditures separately); the actual savings from reduced defense spending; and the ratio of expenditures for education, health, and other social services to defense expenditures. All these indicators should be calculated as averages over a period of three or more years in order to avoid distortions. Finally, the financial multiplier—the ratio of budgetary savings to DRP costs—reveals the amount of savings for each dollar spent on the program.

What the calculation of financial returns cannot provide guidance for is the appropriate level of military expenditure. The size of an army, and hence the size of military expenditures, depends on a country's security environment and its land mass, borders, and population. It is beyond the mandate of a development institution to make judgments about the distribution of expenditures from this broad perspective. However, a developmental perspective does legitimately encompass the sustainability of military expenditure insofar as those expenditures affect macroeconomic stability and reduce spending for the social sectors.

The Impact on Inflation

A DRP can produce inflationary effects in three ways. First, sudden and substantial external funding in foreign currency increases the money supply. The situation worsens when the currency depreciates during implementation. Second, cash payments to ex-combatants, an important element of reinsertion, increase purchasing power, and thus demand, without increasing supply. Third, a United Nations presence to facilitate the peace process leads to a substantial import of foreign exchange.

To help counteract the first problem, the financial aspects of a DRP should be considered within an ongoing stabilization program. Inflationary pressure can also be reduced when donors reallocate funds already designated to the country in order to avoid lengthy program approval procedures.

The inflationary impact of cash payments can also be mitigated, depending on the design of the program. Payments can be made in installments, spreading the cash injections over time. Moreover, as ex-combatants settle across the country, those injections are diffused regionally and the multiplier effects of higher local purchasing power may prevail. No empirical information is yet available on the magnitude and direction of these effects at this point in time.

A strong international presence, especially in a postconflict environment, can have severe effects on the economy. For instance, the United Nations operation in Mozambique cost between $0.7 million and $1.0 million a day. Although much of the budget of the United Nations operation is spent on imports, this injection of foreign exchange inevitably leads to major distortions in markets for nontraded goods (particularly for housing). The United Nations presence in Cambodia had similar effects.

The social consequences are no less grave. Resentment toward United Nations personnel and the proliferation of prostitution are common. The international community therefore needs to be careful that it does not de facto occupy a country and, on its departure, leave behind financial imbalances and social wounds that require years of belt tightening and healing.

Economic Returns

On the one hand, the reintegration of ex-combatants into civil society can place a heavy burden on a country's labor market. On the other hand, ex-combatants, who may number more than 10 percent of the work force, can contribute to economic development by entering into productive, income-generating activities. Only a DRP monitoring system that tracks ex-combatants' employment status, income, and investments can determine their actual contribution to GDP. If such information is not collected, rough estimates must suffice so that at least orders of magnitude can be calculated.

One factor in particular hampers the precise calculation of economic returns: the "crowding out" of civilians in the labor market by ex-combatants. Only a detailed survey can uncover crowding out, and such surveys are seldom feasible because of competing demands on limited resources. The calculations are therefore likely to overestimate the economic returns. Nevertheless, some useful information about the microeconomic impact of DRPs can be gleaned from the following indicators: the income of ex-combatants, factoring in the sector and level of employment; the ratio of ex-combatant income to GDP per capita for the labor force; and the ratio of total ex-combatant income over program benefits (costs). The latter ratio is the economic multiplier of a DRP, which indicates the amount of ex-combatant income triggered by one dollar spent on the program. Again, these indicators should be calculated as averages over a period of three or more years, on the basis of estimates if exact figures are not available.

5
Country Experiences

This chapter pulls together data on programs for demobilization and reintegration from several countries in Sub-Saharan Africa. Case studies on Ethiopia, Namibia, and Uganda are summarized here to allow for detailed comparison. This information is complemented by an analysis of demobilization and reintegration experiences in other countries (Angola, Eritrea, Mozambique, Rwanda, and Zimbabwe), which highlights particular problems and approaches.

Ethiopia, Namibia, and Uganda

The experience of these three countries with DRPs show many similarities despite the different conditions. For example, the reintegration challenges confronting ex-combatants as they sought to adapt to civilian life were clearly similar across all three countries. Ex-combatants' distinct needs and vulnerabilities seem to justify the provision of targeted assistance in the form of demobilization and reintegration programs.

At the same time, the content of program support and the effectiveness of DRP design and implementation differed across the three cases. On a per capita basis, Namibian ex-combatants received the most support and Ethiopian veterans the least. However, the program in Ethiopia is in many ways considered the most successful, that in Namibia the least effective. The Ugandan DRP, which provided extensive assistance to ex-combatants, also achieved most of its objectives.

In many instances, low-cost solutions (for example, skills verification in Ethiopia) may be more effective than costly interventions (such as the elaborate training schemes in Namibia). This general observation suggests that governments and donors cannot "buy success." Rather, the experiences in Ethiopia, Namibia, and Uganda affirm that a successful DRP needs to blend into the political, social, and economic environment, has to be implemented by dedicated and professional staff, and must receive sufficient and timely financial assistance.

Beyond such general comparisons, the field studies of Ethiopia, Namibia, and Uganda provide in-depth information about critical program issues. (A detailed overview is presented in tables 5.1–5.3.) A full report on the DRP programs in these three countries is being published as Colletta and others (forthcoming).

(Text continues on page 65).

Table 5.1 Summary of DRPs in Ethiopia, Namibia, and Uganda

Issue	Ethiopia	Namibia	Uganda
		Political dimensions	
Time frame	Demobilization and reinsertion commenced in June 1991. Reintegration is expected to be completed in 1996.	Demobilization was undertaken in mid-1989. Reinsertion did not start before 1991. Reintegration programs are still ongoing, with no clear deadline.	Demobilization and reinsertion started in December 1992. Reintegration is expected to be completed in late 1997.
Political context	The program took place in the political context of a chaotic transition from war to peace with strong political commitment. Initially, a program was designed by the World Food Programme and the International Labour Organization. After several adaptations, the government firmly took control of the program and its implementation.	The program was part of the larger pacification process under United Nations auspices. A Namibian government did not exist at the time of planning. The incoming government was committed to providing assistance to ex-combatants but lacked expertise and resources. No comprehensive program was ever developed.	The program was a peacetime operation initiated by and enjoying the full support of the government, which has been in control of the entire program.

Table 5.1 (continued)

Issue	Ethiopia	Namibia	Uganda
	Political dimensions (continued)		
National reconciliation	The ethnic strife that fueled the war has not yet been entirely overcome. Problems in some parts of the country (including armed struggle) persist. However, the new government has treated the members of the defeated armies correctly and, in turn, has received their trust.	Ethnic and regional considerations were not concerns during the preparation phase but have since become problems. Ex-combatants of the two erstwhile armies still receive different treatment from government.	When full-fledged war ended in 1986, the victorious forces integrated former opponents into the national army. More than six years later, some communities still rejected ex-combatants if they fought for the "wrong" side.
Key lessons	Political support has been a major factor for successful program implementation despite the program's emergency nature.	Lack of political guidance and incomplete national reconciliation proved problematic for program design and implementation.	Political support has been a major factor in successful program implementation. The fact that the program took place during peacetime allowed for thorough preparation.
	Targeting		
Target groups	In all, over 475,000 combatants of the Derg and Oromo Liberation Front (OLF) have been demobilized. They were the only target group and received assistance regardless of rank. Those who served less than 18 months received only reinsertion support.	Close to 50,000 ex-combatants from both warring factions have been demobilized. They were the only target group and received assistance regardless of rank. Tailored assistance was provided to San Bushmen ex-combatants.	A total of 36,353 soldiers have been demobilized in three phases. Target groups were ex-combatants, spouses, children, and communities.

Identification of beneficiaries	Records existed but were incomplete; arms receipts, salary statements, and comrades' committees were therefore used. An estimated 15 percent of potential beneficiaries have not been reported for identification.	Records for the South-West African Territorial Forces existed. PLAN guerrilla fighters have not been formally identified upon demobilization. They have been registered twice since through comrades' committees.	The army established a comprehensive data base and records system several months before demobilization.
Identification of needs and opportunities	Some qualitative data were collected in the discharge centers, but no profile was developed. No other studies were undertaken.	No study was undertaken.	A socioeconomic profile was developed that formed the basis for another study on program design. A study of the institutional structure was also undertaken.
Socioeconomic profile	Most ex-combatants were under the age of 25 when they joined the Derg army. About half of ex-combatants are married; the rate is higher in rural areas. About half of the ex-combatants have children to support. Most ex-combatants are physically fit. Almost two-thirds of ex-combatants have not gone beyond primary school. An estimated 5 percent of Derg soldiers and 20 percent of OLF ex-fighters are female. Health status is unknown.	Guerrilla ex-combatants have low educational and skills levels. Most joined the army in their twenties and stayed for over ten years. Most are married and have an average of four children. Their health status does not appear worrisome. Up to 30 percent of members of the guerrilla army may have been female; they were mostly engaged in support services.	Perhaps one-third of ex-combatants had joined the movement before age 18. The vast majority are married with, on average, over three children. The health status of almost half of all ex-combatants is poor, and many are assumed to carry the HIV virus. Their educational and skills levels are low. Only a small percentage of ex-combatants are female.

Table 5.1 *(continued)*

Issue	Ethiopia	Namibia	Uganda
	Targeting (continued)		
Development of a targeting mechanism	Ex-combatants were issued identification documents, including a photograph. Leakages have been kept to a minimum.	No special identification document was issued. Throughout the process, leakages have been recurrent, especially for ex-guerrillas.	Ex-combatants were issued discharge certificates, including a photograph. Leakages were practically nonexistent.
Key lessons	A responsive and flexible approach allowed for an effective (although incomplete) method for developing multiple strategies.	The lack of systematic efforts for identifying needs and opportunities led to incomplete program design. These effects were compounded by repeated targeting errors.	The socioeconomic profile allowed for the development of a comprehensive support package. Close adherence to targeting criteria averted leakages.
	Demobilization		
Cantonment and discharge	Ex-combatants reported for assembly in discharge centers in several phases. Assembly lasted for several weeks to a couple of months for Derg ex-combatants, six months for OLF ex-fighters. 130,000 ex-combatants were repatriated from neighboring countries to centers or directly to their home districts.	Guerrilla fighters were demobilized by the United Nations in Angola, but the South-West Africa People's Organization (SWAPO) hid a substantial number of fighters in Angola in case the peace process failed. South-West African troops were demobilized by the South African forces in Namibia. Former counterinsurgency units that had been reassigned to the police, and therefore were not initially demobilized, destabilized several regions until the United Nations forced their disbandment.	Demobilization has taken place in three phases over a three-year period. The soldiers were assembled for very brief periods of less than one week in order to reduce costs and the potential for indiscipline.

48

Disarmament	Derg soldiers were disarmed when returning from Eritrea, when entering discharge centers, or by handing over weapons to community committees. OLF fighters were disamed on defeat. It is estimated that large numbers of weapons are still in circulation outside the army.	Guerilla fighters were disarmed by the United Nations in Angola, and South West African Territorial Forces by the South African forces. It is estimated that large numbers of weapons are still in circulation outside the army.	Soldiers handed over their weapons before leaving the barracks for the discharge centers. It is estimated that large numbers of weapons are still in circulation outside the army.
Predischarge orientation	Predischarge orientation was incomplete because it focused on issues of political reconciliation. This discouraged donors from providing program assistance.	Some limited predischarge orientation was undertaken for both armies, but it was by and large insufficient.	Predischarge orientation programs were enhanced over time and were greatly appreciated by the ex-combatants. The program included environment, health (including AIDS/HIV), legal, and program issues. Wives were targeted in special sessions.
Transportation	Transportation was provided by UNHCR (from abroad) and the Ethiopian Red Cross Society to points close to the ex-combatants' homes. It was executed effectively.	Transportation was provided by UNHCR (from Angola) and the Council of Churches in Namibia (CCN) to points close to the ex-combatants' homes. It was executed effectively.	Transportation to points close to the ex-combatants' homes was arranged by program management and effected mainly by private providers. It was executed effectively.

Table 5.1 *(continued)*

Issue	Ethiopia	Namibia	Uganda
		Demobilization *(continued)*	
Postdischarge orientation	No specific postdischarge orientation about local issues was undertaken.	No specific postdischarge orientation about local issues was undertaken.	A postdischarge orientation program on district-specific opportunities and constraints has been developed for the final phase.
Key lessons	Longer periods of encampment led to discontent and unrest. The provision of information about the challenges of civilian life in a poor country was neglected	Ex-guerrillas had overly optimistic expectations about civilian life because of limited orientation. Holding back or reassigning units, and thus not registering them, created risks for peace and threatened program implementation.	A graduated approach enabled management to improve the quality of implementation and benefits over time, in accordance with the lessons of experience. The predischarge orientation in the later phases proved vital for successful reintegration.

Cash benefits	A one-time cash payment was made to all ex-combatants at the time of discharge. Urban ex-combatants received monthly payments in cash for six to seven months for consumption purposes, depending on army affiliation. The payment was effected through the district offices.	The former South-West African Territorial Forces received their salaries until independence. A one-time cash payment, largely for consumption purposes, was made to unemployed ex-combatants from both sides almost two years after demobilization. The payment was effected through a commercial bank, and leakages were substantial because of lack of records.	Each ex-combatant received a cash payment for consumption and investment, in three installments for phase I and two installments thereafter. The first payment was effected in cash before discharge, the later installments through a commercial bank.
Food allowance	Ex-combatants received food rations in kind for six to ten months, depending on army affiliation and mode of subsistence.	Former guerrilla fighters received food rations in kind for twelve months as part of the refugee resettlement program.	Food expenses for ex-combatants and their families were included in the cash package.
Housing assistance	No specific housing support was offered to ex-combatants. Rural ex-combatants were assisted in accessing land for housing. Communities provided some materials and labor for reconstruction.	The DRP did not include a specific housing component.	Each ex-combatant received twenty iron sheets and ridges as well as other support (in cash equivalent) for materials and labor. The iron sheets were consistently delivered late. Consequently, iron sheets were monetized for phase III ex-combatants.

Table 5.1 (*continued*)

Issue	Ethiopia	Namibia	Uganda
	Reinsertion (*continued*)		
Health support	Each ex-combatant and his or her family receives health support until he or she is considered reintegrated. Costs of medicines are not included.	Health support was extended to ex-combatants between demobilization and independence in March 1990. Since then, they have not received assistance.	Basic health needs for ex-combatants and their families were covered under the cash entitlement. A pilot health care fund was established in phase II, but support was too limited. It was extended thereafter.
Support for children's education	On limited occasions, children received support in the form of school fees and materials through NGOs.	No education support component for children was included in the program.	Two children per ex-combatant were paid school fees for one school year in the first two phases. Many girls were discriminated against in larger families. In phase III, all biological children receive support for the school fees for one year.
Key lessons	The sheer number of ex-combatant beneficiaries precluded more comprehensive reinsertion support. Its design, however, was highly appropriate.	Reinsertion support has been sporadic, uncoordinated, late, and incomplete, contributing to ex-combatant frustration.	Comprehensive reinsertion support was based on a basket of basic needs and minimized discontent. Late delivery of in-kind contributions was the most substantial implementation problem.

Rural support	Access to land has been facilitated for rural settlers. All received tools and equipment. A distinction has been made between cash croppers, food croppers, and pastoralists. Many among the two latter groups received an ox or heifer.	Ex-combatants have been a main target group of the government's resettlement program. They receive land, production assistance, food, and other basic needs.	All ex-combatants received a cash equivalent for the purchase of seeds and tools. Access to land was facilitated through the involvement of local communities.
Urban support	Employment support, formal education, vocational training, skills certification, placement, and credit services were offered. The credit scheme operates on a grant basis, and its sustainability criteria include social and political concerns.	The training offered to ex-combatants is supply driven and in general does not meet the requirements of the labor market. Most trainers lack qualifications. The program is expensive.	A training program has been introduced in phase II, consisting of formal education, vocational training, and apprenticeship training. Information and counseling have received increasing attention during implementation, including referrals to ongoing small-scale credit and grants programs in a limited number of districts.
Program for the disabled	Three programs have been designed for less severely, moderately, and more severely disabled ex-combatants. The latter two groups receive institutional care. All but the most needy will eventually be integrated.	Disabled ex-combatants are eligible for the government's rehabilitation program. It is not known how many of them have been covered thus far.	Severely disabled ex-combatants are eligible for special treatment. However, their numbers were underestimated, and coverage has been extended for phase III.

Table 5.1 *(continued)*

Issue	Ethiopia	Namibia	Uganda
		Reintegration (continued)	
Pension scheme	Eligible ex-combatants are covered under the government's pension scheme. With the exception of the disabled, those eligible for pensions have not received any other support.	A small number of ex-combatants from both armies are eligible for pensions.	A pension and gratuity scheme has been developed outside the program, especially for former officers, to compensate them for the unitary package.
Program for women	No special efforts were undertaken to facilitate reintegration of spouses and female ex-combatants.	No special efforts were undertaken to facilitate reintegration of spouses and female ex-combatants.	In the initial phase, an ongoing small-scale credit program was extended to cover wives and female ex-combatants, but it produced few results. In the final phase, female ex-combatants and wives of severely disabled ex-combatants are afforded preferential access to training.
Key lessons	The design of multiple strategies on the basis of the mode of subsistence was exemplary and effectively assisted the reintegration of the majority of ex-combatants.	Resettlement and rehabilitation support have not yet been able to facilitate the self-sufficiency of beneficiaries. The training program is largely ineffective. Benefits have been unevenly distributed among ex-combatants.	Initially this was a reinsertion program, but pilot reintegration components have been added with qualified success. Although not all-encompassing, the gender focus was the strongest of any program thus far.

Social dimensions

Psychological reintegration	No detailed information is available, but psychological reintegration does not seem to have posed serious problems.	Many ex-combatants lack a purpose in life and have developed a dependency syndrome. Some are under severe mental stress.	By and large, ex-combatants have mastered reintegration without psychological problems.
Mutual support	Most ex-combatants meet their former comrades regularly or occasionally. They help and counsel each other.	Ex-combatants have developed informal networks. They jointly work on economic projects or on the fields.	Ex-combatants have formed a large number of groups and jointly undertake economic projects. They provide each other with information and counseling.
Land and housing	Most rural ex-combatants were able to access land through government support. About half the ex-combatants own a house, which significantly helped reintegration.	Many ex-combatants found access to land a major problem.	Of phase I and II ex-combatants, less than 10 percent did not have access to land, but approximately 40 percent did not have a house and had to stay with relatives or friends temporarily.
Crime and antisocial behavior	No significant relationship exists between the increase in crime and the number of ex-combatants in a community. Most ex-combatants are disciplined.	Criminal acts by ex-combatants are infrequent.	Crime committed by ex-combatants has been negligible. Only some 10 percent are considered undisciplined troublemakers, drug abusers, or thieves.
Divorce and marriage rates	Domestic violence and divorce rates among ex-combatants are similar to those of the rest of the population. Many ex-combatants married after their return.	No information is available.	Up to 50 percent of ex-combatants may have divorced after returning home. A substantial number married a second wife after divorce.

Table 5.1 (*continued*)

Issue	Ethiopia	Namibia	Uganda
	Social dimensions (*continued*)		
Women's isolation	The more the ex-combatants participated in community activities, the better was the acceptance of the spouse and family.	No information is available.	Almost one-fifth of marriages have not been formalized. Over 15 percent of wives do not speak the local language at the place of settlement.
Community sensitization	Peace and stability committees have been created by government to further reconciliation. Community leaders are well informed about the program.	The CCN established repatriation committees, but its mandate did not explicitly include ex-combatant reintegration. The government did not undertake specific efforts.	Sensitization tours were conducted regularly, but their impact on community sensitization was limited. A social communication component has therefore been introduced in phase III.
Community acceptance	Most ex-combatants joined their old communities and were therefore generally received well, especially when they participated in community activities.	Most ex-combatants joined their old communities. Community acceptance commonly depended on the ethnic background and army affiliation of the ex-combatant. In some cases, communities expect repentence. Overall, ex-combatants have been treated fairly.	Most ex-combatants joined their old communities. By and large, ex-combatants were welcomed by their communities. Some communities resented the special assistance, and a few others still see ex-combatants as traitors. Stigmatization became a problem and led to a change in terminology.

Key lessons	Having fought for the defeated army, ex-combatants generally had limited expectations. Active participation in community life facilitated social reintegration. The use of existing social capital by building on Derg-inspired organizations to reallocate formerly collective lands to ex-combatants was a critical factor. Communities were well aware of issues.	Ex-combatants were not helped to lower their expectations, nor were communities aided in the social reintegration process. Full social reintegration can only be achieved with complete national reconciliation.	Serious problems have been encountered by wives who were from a different ethnic background than their husbands. Generally, community acceptance was good, with the exception of initial resentment in the north of the country.

Institutional structure

Institutional structure	A demobilization and reintegration commission was created under an advisory committee for overall implementation and coordination. Transaction costs have been limited to below 9 percent of total program costs.	Resettlement and rehabilitation were part of regular government programs. The Development Brigade Corporation (DBC) was created to train ex-combatants. Transaction costs have been very high, surpassing 50 percent for resettlement projects.	A secretariat for implementation was established under a board. Transaction costs have been limited to just above 8 percent of program costs.
Field representation and decentralization	The commission had 36 district offices and seven regional offices with an adequate degree of autonomy. Quarterly coordination meetings were held.	Although district-level authorities were involved, decisionmaking remained centralized and politicized.	The secretariat has 38 district offices with some degree of autonomy. Headquarters and district staff lacked mobility. Coordination meetings were held infrequently.
Community and beneficiary involvement	District officials were involved in decisionmaking through local advisory and other committees. Communities have received repeated attention. Ex-combatants elected their representatives as members of committees.	On selected occasions, community and church representatives were involved but without proper planning. Ex-combatants remained passive beneficiaries.	District advisory committees have been created, comprising district officials. Communities have received limited attention. Ex-combatants elected their representatives as members of committees and to assist district-based staff.

Table 5.1 *(continued)*

Issue	Ethiopia	Namibia	Uganda
	Institutional structure (continued)		
Key lessons	Central coordination and decentralized implementation, as well as community and beneficiary participation, have been exemplary.	Uncoordinated implementation of various components led to duplication and high transaction costs. Centralization negatively affected staff morale.	Outreach activities have been limited, but field representation, decentralization, and the participation of ex-combatants proved very useful.
	Management aspects		
Staffing	Ex-combatants were used as outreach staff. Training was limited, but staff were highly motivated.	Regular government staff were charged with the resettlement and rehabilitation programs. The DBC employed a large number of ex-combatants without proper qualifications.	Most of the central staff have been ex-combatants. In the district offices, regular administration staff were seconded to the veterans' assistance program. Staff received continuous training throughout implementation.
Monitoring, reporting, and evaluation	Reporting was undertaken regularly at the district level, monitoring at the central level. An ex-post, small-scale impact evaluation was funded by donors.	Detailed monitoring and reporting have been neglected. An ex-post, small-scale impact evaluation was funded by donors.	A management information system was installed with several initial problems. Once fully developed, monitoring and reporting were performed at a satisfactory level, although some district staff remained passive. Independent, in-depth evaluations have been undertaken.

Accounting and auditing	Accounting procedures were followed properly. An internal auditing unit has been established.	Accounting has been weak, especially in the DBC. A government audit on the DBC has been undertaken recently.	Accounting procedures were followed meticulously. An external auditing firm undertook monthly audits.
Key lessons	Staff motivation was essential for implementation.	Lack of staff motivation and qualifications rendered many services ineffective. The lack of monitoring and accounting led to misuse of funds.	The management information system and accounting and auditing procedures have been exemplary and were major factors in smooth operations and donor support.

External assistance

Strategies and timelines	The UNHCR and ICRC were instrumental during the demobilization process. Initially, donors were hesitant because they had doubts about the government's implementation capacity and feared that the cantonment phase would be politicized. Most development donors were unable to respond to emergency needs, and most support was forthcoming only after lengthy delays.	The UNHCR and ICRC were instrumental during the demobilization process. In the initial reintegration phase, one donor actively supported the development of the training program but soon withdrew almost all its support. Donors have not played a conspicuously constructive role in the process.	Donors treated the DRP as a restructuring of public expenditures cum social safety net. Demobilization criteria were transparent, and the donor community provided considerable assistance. Later, donors added political conditionalities to aid and focused more on reintegration. Funding delays were common.

Table 5.1 *(continued)*

Issue	Ethiopia	Namibia	Uganda
	External assistance (continued)		
Purpose of support	Several donors and NGOs started independent parallel projects. The initial lead agency was accused of furthering its own interest, and it finally withdrew. A major donor provided tied but inappropriate aid.	Several donors provided specific support to the DRP but not necessarily through government.	Most donors provided support to the overall program. A major donor provided tied aid that proved expensive and late.
Coordination	Initially, donors had regular meetings with government, but these were discontinued when it became clear that donors would not be able to provide comprehensive support. The German technical cooperation agency (GTZ) supported the commission by implementing its own reintegration program for ex-servicemen and displaced persons. The U.S. Agency for International Development also financed operational and logistical support to the commission.	Demobilization was undertaken practically without government involvement. Donor and NGO support was largely uncoordinated, both among themselves and vis-à-vis the government.	The World Bank, as the lead agency, effectively coordinated donor support. Relations with the government during implementation were exceptionally good. Donors and government jointly developed the individual program phases.
Key lessons	Emergency assistance proved valuable. However, lack of a donor strategy on reintegration seriously threatened the program's financial viability. Relations between government and many donors have ranged from indifferent to highly problematic.	Emergency assistance proved valuable, as no government was yet in place. Later, donors sent mixed signals to government about their interests and suspended support at a critical stage.	Government-donor relations were exemplary. The coordination of donor support by one lead agency proved crucial. Program ownership was mutual.

Table 5.2 Estimated Program Costs and Financing

Item	Ethiopia Dollars	Ethiopia Percent	Namibia Dollars	Namibia Percent	Uganda Dollars	Uganda Percent
Program costs[a]	195,500,000	100.0	41,270,000	100.0	40,494,790	100.0
Demobilization[b]	n.a.	32.9	n.a.	—	3,279,158	8.1
Reinsertion	n.a.	33.0	8,000,000	19.4	30,270,428	74.8
Reintegration	n.a.	25.5	33,270,000	80.6	2,292,652	5.7
Administration[c]	n.a.	8.6	n.a.	—	3,897,441	9.6
Costs per ex-combatant	411	—	1,263	—	1,114	—
Ratio of costs per ex-combatant to per capita GDP[e]	—	0.5	—	0.1	—	0.8
Funding[f]	195,500,000	100.0	41,270,000	100.0	43,210,822	100.0
Government	67,600,000	43.8	20,138,200	48.8	4,869,391	11.3
Multilaterals	41,200,000	17.2	n.a.	—	4,200,195	9.7
Bilaterals[g]	56,400,000	26.9	21,131,800	51.2	34,141,236	79.0
NGOs	30,200,000	12.2	n.a.	—	0	0.0

n.a. Not available.

— Not applicable.

Note: Exchange rates: for Ethiopia, ETB 2.07 per dollar during demobilization and reinsertion and 25 percent of administration, ETB 5 per dollar during reintegration; for Namibia, N$ 3 per dollar; for Uganda, USh 1,000 per dollar.

a. Budgeted amounts in Uganda, including contingencies; actual program costs not yet available.

b. Breakdown not possible because of exchange rate fluctuation for Ethiopia. Demobilization in Namibia was budgeted under the United Nations Transitory Assistance Group (UNTAG), UNHCR, CCN and other key players. No information is available.

c. Included in reinsertion and reintegration for Namibia.

d. Per capita GDP for the economically active population during the first two and a half years after demobilization (reinsertion in Namibia).

e. Per capita GDP for economically active population during program period. For Uganda, phases I and II only.

f. For Uganda, receipts for phases I and II and pledges for phase III. Expenditures and receipts differ for each phase.

g. Includes multilateral donors and NGOs for Namibia.

Source: Ethiopian Commission for the Rehabilitation of Members of the Former Army and Disabled War Veterans; Government of Namibia budget documents; Uganda Veterans Assistance Board; World Bank staff estimates.

61

Table 5.3 Estimated Economic Impact of Transition from War to Peace

Item	Ethiopia	Namibia	Uganda[a]
Economic loss[b]			
GDP war growth rate (percent)[c]	-1.2	2.6	1.7
GDP postwar growth rate (percent)[d]	6.7	3.9	5.8
Average annual loss due to war (millions of dollars)[e]	956.1	36.8	14.8
Average annual loss as percentage of GDP at factor cost or basic prices	18.4	1.9	8.1
DRP costs in relation to average annual loss (ratio)[f]	0.20	1.12	2.74
Financial returns[b]			
Defense expenditures as percentage of total government expenditures[g]	46.6; 16.4	12.4; 6.3	34.9; 25.0
Budgetary savings as percentage of total government expenditures[h]	30.2	6.1	9.9
Social expenditures in relation to defense expenditures (ratio)[g]	0.4; 1.4	2.8; 7.2	0.7; 1.1
Budgetary savings in relation to DRP costs (financial multiplier ratio)	5.21	3.57	0.92
Economic returns[i]			
Ex-combatants as percentage of labor force	2.25	11.79	0.18
Annual average income per ex-combatant (dollars)[j]	129	1,527	187; 203
Annual average income per ex-combatant as percentage of per capita GDP[k]	55.4	35.5	36.6; 41.0
Total ex-combatant income in relation to DRP costs (economic multiplier ratio)	1.59	0.78	0.37
Employment status after demobilization (percent, except as indicated)			
Agriculture[l]	65.0	40.0	77.0
Unskilled[m]	—	15.0	13.0
Skilled	15.0	7.0	—
Professional	5.0	3.0	—
Unemployed[n]	15.0	35.0	10.0
Ex-combatants demobilized (number)[f]	475,759	49,500	36,358

Item	Ethiopia	Namibia	Uganda[a]
Economic reintegration	The majority of ex-combatants seem to be poorer than their civilian neighbors; their income may reach no more than 50 percent of average earnings (detailed employment or income data do not exist).	Generally, ex-combatants remain a vulnerable group among the poor, even many of those who had received training or resettlement support. Their income may be as low as one-third of average earnings (detailed employment or income data do not exist).	Most combatants joined the ranks of the poor upon demobilization. They may earn less than half of average incomes (income data do not exist).
Synopsis	Because of the high wartime expenditures on defense, the budgetary savings and the financial multiplier of the transition from war to peace, including the DRP were substantial. Per capita costs were equal to half the average income. Worn out by a prolonged war, the defeated Derg soldiers have generally accepted a limited but still comprehensive support package.	Because most wartime expenses were incurred outside Namibia (PLAN, People's Liberation Army Namibia supporters and South Africa), the budgetary savings were limited. Nevertheless, the financial multiplier was high, because the DRP was part of the broader transition from war to peace. Ex-combatants represented 12 percent of the labor force, and their return had an extensive impact on the labor market. Per capita costs were only one-tenth of the average income. Moreover, benefits were unevenly distributed, with 7 percent of ex-combatants receiving 72 percent of benefits. The victorious ex-guerrilla fighters expected more comprehensive support, hence discontent persisted.	The financial and economic multipliers were low because of the free-standing nature of the DRP. Per capita costs reached about 80 percent of the average income. The support measures generally enabled members of a victorious and unified army to reintegrate well. The program also benefited from the general availability of land as the key production factor in the country, as well as from a low ratio of ex-combatants in the total labor force.

63

Table 5.3 *(continued)*

a. For Uganda, phases I and II only, covering 32,211 ex-combatants.
b. In real terms. Ethiopia, 1980–81 = 100; Namibia, 1992 = 100; Uganda, 1991 = 100.
c. Three-year average before demobilization, plus the first postwar year during which economic activity has not yet recovered.
d. Four-year average one year after demobilization; two-year average for Ethiopia.
e. Assuming the economy grew at the postwar rate during the last three years of war, plus the first postwar year, and comparing this potential GDP with actual GDP.
f. All phases for Uganda.
g. Three-year averages before and after demobilization.
h. Budgetary savings refer to government savings from reduced military expenditures.
i. In nominal terms since discharge. For Namibia program costs in relation to income ratio between 1991–92 and 1993–94. For Uganda phases I and II separately.
j. ETB 5 per dollar, N$ 3 per dollar, USh 1,000 per dollar.
k. Per capita GDP for the economically active population.
l. Ethiopia includes unskilled. Uganda includes family and casual labor.
m. Uganda includes nonagricultural employment and self-employment.
n. The definition of unemployment varies by country. For instance, people engaged in subsistence agriculture are considered unemployed in Namibia. For Uganda, the unemployed include unpaid family workers.
Source: National Ministries of Finance; Sitari and others (1995); Woldu (1995); Uganda Veterans Assistance Board; World Bank staff estimates.

64

Other Countries

The demobilization and reintegration programs undertaken in several other countries in Sub-Saharan Africa contain elements similar to those of programs in Ethiopia, Namibia, and Uganda, and they face similar problems. They do, however, exhibit unique features, the analysis of which demonstrates the complexity of DRPs. The experiences of the five countries reviewed here—Angola, Eritrea, Mozambique, Rwanda, and Zimbabwe—thus complement the findings from the three case studies.

Angola: Demobilization Reactivated

The Lisbon agreement of May 31, 1991, brokered by Portugal with the support of the United States and the Soviet Union, officially ended the sixteen-year civil war between the government (Movimento Popular de Libertação de Angola) and the guerrilla forces of UNITA (União Nacional para a Independêcia Total de Angola). This agreement foresaw a ceasefire, the integration of the two armies, and multiparty elections in late 1992. In preparation for demobilization, which was to precede army integration, a socioeconomic survey was conducted on the government forces but not on UNITA fighters. With those data in hand, preparation of reintegration measures commenced.

Overall, the demobilization process was poorly managed and monitored by the United Nations Angola Verification Mission. By mid-1992 most UNITA troops had been encamped, but many fighters remained hidden in the bush. The encamped troops were assembled with their families, and their living conditions were acceptable. One year after the peace accord, just over a third of the regular army had been encamped, living conditions had deteriorated, and the desertion rate was high. Moreover, weapons were poorly stored and guarded in these camps; in effect, the encamped fighters had access to arms.

Demobilization itself started before encampment was complete, but it remained unfinished at election time. The DRP process thus contributed significantly to insecurity, and when the elections brought victory for the MPLA government, UNITA leaders refused to accept the results. They chose to recommence their armed struggle in 1993, in an attempt to gain with bullets what they had lost at the ballot box.

It took another year and a half for the government and UNITA to sign a new peace pact, and only after a meeting of the leaders of the two parties in May 1995 did national reconciliation move forward significantly. Coordination between the two warring factions is now much improved in some respects (in the areas of humanitarian assistance and demining, for example).

By July 1995 the government and UNITA had settled on procedures for demobilization and reintegration, and the United Nations Humanitarian Program for Demobilization and Reintegration had been reviewed and revised within the United Nations Consolidated Inter-Agency Appeal for Angola. The operational framework encompasses four stages: quartering of UNITA military personnel, global incorporation of UNITA fighters into the national armed forces, demobilization, and reintegration. The whole process is scheduled to take close to two and a half years.

Health and civic training programs are planned during the quartering phase, in addition to provision of food and distribution of household kits. Reintegration will focus on training and quick-impact income-generation projects. These projects are expected to be implemented in a timely manner, have a high impact, be capable of multiplying their effects, and cover a wide array of ex-combatants' needs. Preparatory studies and ex-combatant profiles undertaken during the encampment phase will determine the specific content of these reintegration components.

Concurrently the World Bank has financed a social action project, with ex-combatants as a major target group. The Angolan operation, which will demobilize and reintegrate approximately 100,000 ex-combatants from both sides, is a highly complex endeavor. Many donors are participating in its implementation, yet the local capacity for implementation remains limited, the quartering process has been grindingly slow, and the political will to implement the peace has been questionable.

Eritrea: Reintegration Blues

The Eritrean People's Liberation Front (EPLF) successfully seized power in Eritrea in 1991 after a thirty-year war of secession against the Ethiopian state. As part of a broader national reconstruction strategy with a focus on social and economic development, the EPLF decided to reduce the liberation army by 50–60 percent from 1993 onward. To date, the EPLF has demobilized 48,000 fighters (half of its forces) in two phases without significant external assistance. The fighters received a cash payment corresponding to their length of service, financial assistance and food rations for a one-year period, and assurances of sustained reintegration support.

In recognition that demobilized fighters will need some long-term assistance with reintegration, the EPLF also established the Department of Reintegration for Demobilized Fighters (Mitias). Mitias, a semi-autonomous body, shares with the parastatal Eritrean Relief and Rehabilitation Agency the mandate of coordinating all social and economic reintegration activities in close cooperation with implementing bodies.

The task facing Mitias is daunting: the economy has yet to recover from the effects of many years of warfare and mismanagement, and the victorious ex-fighters have high expectations. Urban and rural unemployment rates are very high, training opportunities are limited, and adequate housing is scarce. Furthermore, the ex-fighters have to compete with 650,000 civilian returnees and people who had been internally displaced. Only 7,000 ex-fighters so far have secured permanent employment, and many reside in temporary shelters, unable to afford permanent housing.

The EPLF had more women—25 to 30 percent—among its ranks than any other liberation army in Sub-Saharan Africa. More than half of those women have children. Despite their comparatively high literacy rate and their demonstrated commitment to the quest for a better future, their economic reintegration is hampered by inadequate child-care support. Furthermore, having gained a great degree of equality and independence in the liberation forces, they are struggling to reintegrate socially into what largely remains a patriarchal society.

The pragmatic and much-lauded efforts of Mitias to provide microlevel support for reintegration in agriculture, marine resources, and vocational training have been constrained by a shortage of effective international assistance and associated funds and by inadequate project planning and management capacity. The Eritrean government's assertive approach to negotiations, coupled with procedural delays in donor bureaucracies, has led to reduced donor support. Coordination between Mitias and donors has improved, however, and Mitias plans to provide more assistance at the microlevel with help from donors and NGOs. Mitias also plans to support the development of small enterprises and to provide counseling and guidance.

Mozambique: Piecemeal Reintegration

The signing of the general peace accord in 1993 by FRELIMO (Frente de Libertação de Moçambique) and RENAMO (Resistência Nacional Moçambicano) brought an end to twenty-eight years of civil warfare in Mozambique. The implementation of the peace process was monitored and largely managed by the United Nations Operation for Mozambique (UNOMOZ), which consisted of 7,500 military personnel. The United Nations operations cost approximately $700,000 to $1 million per day.

Demobilization of the estimated 100,000 government and guerrilla forces by UNOMOZ was a key component of the peace process preceding the elections. Demobilization was divided into four phases: cantonment, registration, disarmament, and transportation of ex-combatants and their dependents. The two parties were to select 30,000 volunteers to join the new national army, but only 11,000 ex-combatants eventually volunteered.

According to the peace accord, the operation was to last five months and to be concluded by April 15, 1994, six months before the elections. Mutual lack of trust between the parties, the slow arrival of UNOMOZ military contingents, and RENAMO's attempt to exploit the process to gain financial and security concessions from UNOMOZ delayed the completion of demobilization.

The slow pace of cantonment led to overcrowding. Living conditions deteriorated in some camps, which in turn contributed to unrest, looting, and banditry. Furthermore, the continued presence of armed forces awaiting demobilization undermined free campaigning on several occasions. Demobilization was finally completed in August 1994.

The national social and economic context for reintegration is bleak: social capital has been diminished after so many years of bitter warfare; 4 million civilian returnees seek resettlement; much of the national infrastructure has been destroyed; landmines inhibit resettlement and agriculture in many areas; unemployment is very high; and the government's capacity to provide effective assistance is limited. The perception that veterans pose a threat to local and regional security is widespread.

Under the terms of the peace accord, the Commission for Reintegration was established under United Nations chairmanship to design and coordinate social and economic reintegration programs until the expiration of the UNOMOZ mandate in December 1994. Skepticism about the government's implementation capacity and accountability has led donors to develop and implement support programs without much government involvement.

These support programs include a transitional safety net for the ex-combatants, which consists of two years' salary (dependent on rank and not tied to inflation), civilian clothing, agricultural inputs, and transportation to the preferred location of resettlement. In addition, donors are promoting a multipronged reintegration strategy comprising an interlinked information referral system, a training fund, and a provincial fund for community-based microprojects. By mid-1995 donors had assisted 13,000 ex-combatants in nearly 550 activities; by the end of 1996 support will be extended to another 15,000 beneficiaries.

Only recently did the government create the National Commission for Social Reinsertion, led by the Ministry of Social Action (which is charged with overall program coordination). The Bank's contribution focuses on strengthening central and local coordination and implementation of training and employment generation, in addition to providing financial support to ongoing donor programs.

Rwanda: Demobilization Derailed

After a prolonged and inconclusive military struggle, the government of the Republic of Rwanda and the Rwandese Patriotic Front signed a peace accord in August 1993. The accord included measures for the demobilization and reintegration of 36,700 members of military and police forces who would not be incorporated into the new unified National Army and National Gendarmerie.

The demobilization of these forces was to be an important component of the transition to a peaceful society and economy. At Rwanda's request—and in the context of the country's planned macroeconomic adjustment program—a World Bank mission in January–February 1994 linked with donors already active in the planning process and drafted a proposal for a Rwandan Demobilization and Reintegration Program (RDRP).

The assembly and cantonment of soldiers designated for demobilization was to commence soon after a broad-based transitional government had been established; operations were to be jointly managed and financed by the transitional government and the United Nations Mission in Rwanda. Reinsertion and reintegration were to be implemented by a civilian Veterans' Coordination Committee, which was to be chaired by the secretary of state for rehabilitation and social integration and composed of representatives of relevant line ministries. The international community and NGOs were to supply financial and technical assistance.

The national social and economic context presented several challenges to the reinsertion and reintegration phases of the RDRP. For example, Rwandan social capital was very weak after decades of ethnic conflict, and the need for confidence-building policies of reconciliation was great. Furthermore, Rwanda possessed the highest ratio of population to land density in Sub-Saharan Africa, limiting the potential for large-scale reintegration in the agricultural sector, and urban employment opportunities had narrowed in the wake of the disruptive civil war. Program designers therefore sought to promote urban microenterprises and to give veterans temporary training and educational opportunities while the economy recovered and the labor market improved.

The RDRP consisted of the following components: a core package that was to provide veterans with the means to satisfy their basic needs (especially for housing, clothing, food, and medical expenses) for a nine-month period; a transitional allowance pegged to rank that was to supply cash for other needs; a counseling and placement service that was to advise veterans about their opportunities in civilian life, facilitate their participation in appropriate training and educational programs, and place them with relevant employers; a children's education fund;

and a veterans' education and training scholarship fund. Detailed surveys concerning land, training, education, and labor markets were to complement the envisaged final proposal.

Implementation of the RDRP was preempted by the tragic turn of internal political events in Rwanda two months after the Bank mission. Recently, the government of Rwanda has again requested the Bank's leadership in DRP design, with reconciliation measures to be included as part of the overall program.

Zimbabwe: Reintegration Revisited

The Lancaster House agreement of 1979 signaled the end of a protracted civil war for independence in Zimbabwe (formerly Rhodesia). Demobilization of the military forces of the three parties—15,000 soldiers of the white Rhodesian government, 30,000 fighters of the Zimbabwe African National Union (ZANU), and 20,000 fighters of the Zimbabwe African People's Union (ZAPU)—was an integral part of the peace process that succeeded the conflict.

A monitoring force of 1,300 from the British Commonwealth supervised the preindependence process; it organized the assembly and cantonment of the ZANU and ZAPU forces and the confinement to barracks of Rhodesian armed forces. The newly established Joint High Command then administered the assembled forces and provided free rations, accommodations, and a monthly allowance. However, up to 15,000 guerrilla fighters reportedly did not enter the camps but were instead retained outside Zimbabwe borders by ZANU and ZAPU, ready for recall if the peace process failed.

Of the 65,000 encamped ex-combatants, 29,000 were integrated in the new armed forces and 36,000 were discharged and received reintegration assistance. Another 22,300 fighters who had been kept across the border or who had been inactive at the time of the agreement were deemed eligible for reintegration assistance. The reintegration schemes for ex-guerrillas and ex-Rhodesian forces differed substantially. Nonconscripts in the Rhodesian army received social benefits and pension plans, but conscripts, who had served only a short time and who had always been expected to return to civilian life, were ineligible for benefits.

In an attempt to quell growing frustration within the assembly camps and to encourage ex-combatants to return to civilian life, the government promised reintegration assistance: counseling and employment support, educational and vocational training, and a significant monthly demobilization allowance. In practice, no employment counseling system was implemented, and vocational training and health care assistance were provided almost exclusively by local NGOs with foreign funding. The most effective NGO was the Zimbabwe Project, which by 1984 had supported income-generating projects and training for about 10,000 ex-combatants. A clear lesson of the Zimbabwean experience with vocational training is that it needs to be followed up by employment referral and counseling.

The government gave veterans cash payments, employed 10,000 ex-combatants in the civil service and in the military (by 1992 the national army consisted of 54,500 soldiers), helped an unknown number of soldiers obtain land, and administered an education scholarship fund for 3,400 veterans. Nevertheless, although the government spent $3,067 per former guerrilla, the economic reintegration of ex-combatants has been less successful than had been hoped. By 1988 only 10 percent of ex-combatants were formally employed or self-employed in the private sector.

Now that apartheid has ended in South Africa, the Mozambican civil war is over, and the government has adopted economic adjustment policies, Zimbabwe is considering a new round of demobilization. The country hopes to reduce its military expenditures and reap the benefits of improved regional security.

6
Conclusion

For the past three decades civil wars have destroyed African lives, skills, and assets, undermined institutional competence and accountability, caused incalculable personal dislocation and suffering, and intensified ethnic hostilities. In sum, internal strife has wrought havoc on civil society throughout much of the region.

There is now little doubt, from the Horn to the Cape, that development in Sub-Saharan Africa cannot be sustained without political stability and underlying security. Orderly demobilization, reinsertion, and reintegration of military personnel are central contributions to the restoration of civil society and the peaceful return to productive civilian life of hitherto destabilizing forces. Equally important are the establishment of a transparent legal system, a professional police force, and an independent judiciary and the implementation of economic reforms aimed at promoting growth and expanding employment opportunities.

Operational experience and field research have enlarged our conceptualization of the technical aspects of DRPs. We can now identify at least three interwoven technical phases of any DRP: demobilization, including disarmament and discharge; reinsertion, including resettlement; and reintegration. Our analysis has also brought into clearer focus the need for two more dimensions in the transition from war to peace—prevention and reconciliation (figure 6.1).

Prevention: Arms and Development

Overall, arms exports to Sub-Saharan Africa have declined markedly since the late 1980s, but sales of small weapons, especially antipersonnel mines, continue to be a lucrative business. The use of such weapons results in a most inhumane form of warfare that affects the civilian population more than it does the fighting army. For example, the estimated 100 million landmines spread across sixty countries kill 24,000 people each year, mostly in developing countries. About 20 million mines carpet several countries in Sub-Saharan Africa. Between 8 million and 10 million mines and unexploded ordnance are deployed in Angola alone.

It costs nearly $1,000 to deactivate a mine costing as little as $3 to purchase. Worse yet, the mere threat of these mines has hampered market forces—the movement of people, goods, and services—and

the resettlement of large tracts of arable land. Agricultural development has been retarded across Africa. The donor community may be·
able to accelerate the pace of demining by increasing funding and
promoting new mine-clearing technology, but in the long run the manu-
facture and sale of small arms must be reduced if development is to
be sustained. The negative connection between arms proliferation and
protracted insecurity, on the one hand, and sustainable development,
on the other, is self-evident.

The Conference on the Convention on Conventional Weapons, held
in November 1995 in Vienna, addressed this issue. It was unable to
reach consensus on a reform of the global governance regime for land
mines. Discussions continue in capitals around the world. A laudable
effort has also been launched by Nobel peace laureate Oscar S. Arias. In
Human Development Report 1994, a publication of the United Nations
Development Programme, he proposed a Global Demilitarization Fund
that would finance activities from demining to demobilization. Such
efforts deserve the support of the development community.

Reconciliation: From War-Torn to Civil Society

At the other end of this seamless web of war-to-peace transition, reintegration in its full sense implies reentry into political and social as well
as economic life. One of the legacies of protracted civil strife, however—
in addition to the destruction of physical and human capital—has been
the displacement of millions of people and the debasement of social
capital. Of the estimated 70 million displaced persons in the world,
about half are in Sub-Saharan Africa. More than a fifth of the people in
nine African countries are displaced, as is a staggering two-thirds of
Liberia's population.

Social capital goes beyond the basic level of human association and
trust that welds a civil society together; it also encompasses organizations, networks, and unwritten mores and rules. Field data for all three
country case studies point to the importance of social support—be it
family, religious groups, or ex-combatants themselves—in easing the
reintegration process. Such social support provides not only
psychosocial sustenance to returnees but also the pathways for becoming economically productive members of society (via information and financial assistance, among other critical things).

Rebuilding social capital means a revitalization of civil society, and
revitalizing civil society entails the promotion of local associations, community participation, and peer accountability. It reduces the level of
individual fear, enables the collective censure of violence, and promotes
local security. These are minimal conditions that must be met if people

Figure 6.1 The Seamless Web of Transition from War to Peace

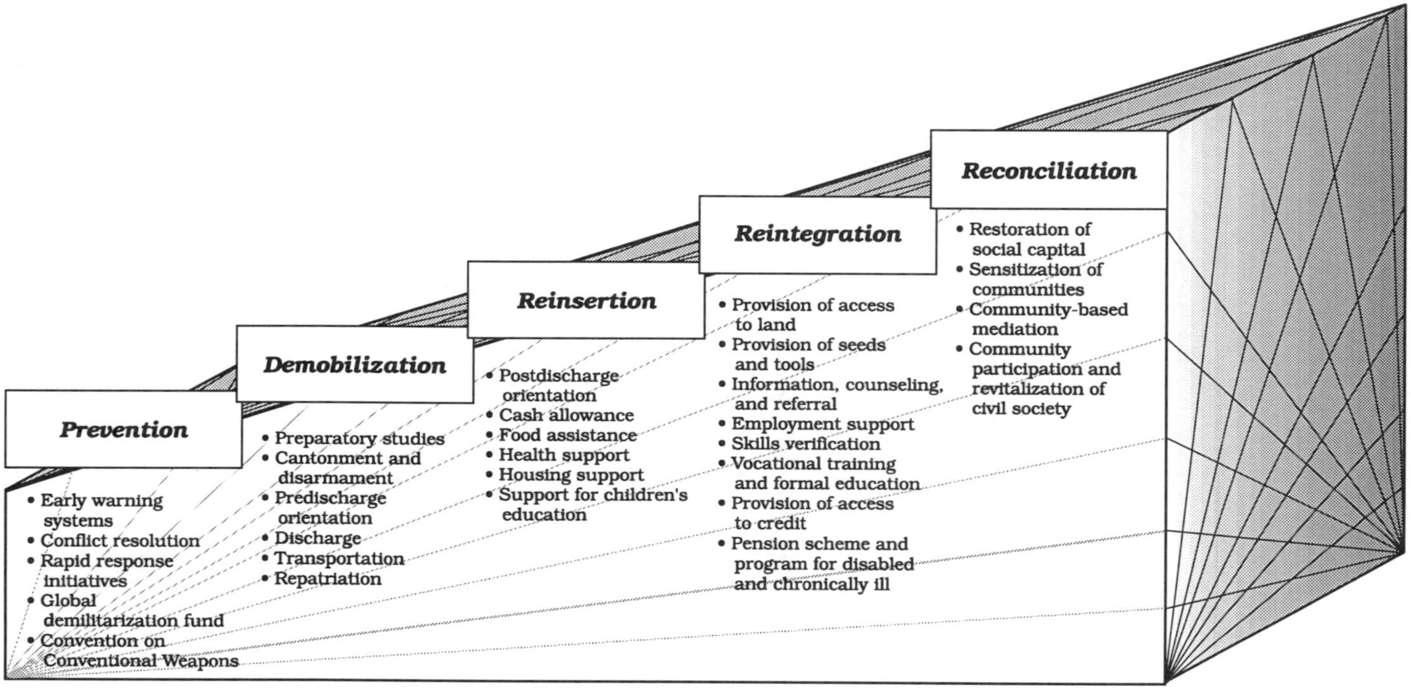

Prevention
- Early warning systems
- Conflict resolution
- Rapid response initiatives
- Global demilitarization fund
- Convention on Conventional Weapons

Demobilization
- Preparatory studies
- Cantonment and disarmament
- Predischarge orientation
- Discharge
- Transportation
- Repatriation

Reinsertion
- Postdischarge orientation
- Cash allowance
- Food assistance
- Health support
- Housing support
- Support for children's education

Reintegration
- Provision of access to land
- Provision of seeds and tools
- Information, counseling, and referral
- Employment support
- Skills verification
- Vocational training and formal education
- Provision of access to credit
- Pension scheme and program for disabled and chronically ill

Reconciliation
- Restoration of social capital
- Sensitization of communities
- Community-based mediation
- Community participation and revitalization of civil society

are to reinvest in their communities, emotionally and financially. The state of social capital is also a barometer for external investors.

When it comes to reintegration, donors have a role beyond promoting employment and training for ex-combatants or rebuilding service structures. This role is the promotion of civil society. In many fragile sociopolitical environments, NGOs and secular and religious groups are at work organizing reconciliation activities, open community meetings, and other activities for free and transparent public exchanges between formerly hostile groups and individuals.

In Namibia church-led repatriation committees rebuilt trust between former adversaries in combat, now neighbors in development. In Somalia, in an attempt to rebuild civil society in the wake of the breakdown of bureaucratic authority, NGOs are working to reestablish the council of elders as a time-tested means of interclan governance. In South Africa a Truth Commission is trying to heal the wounds of years of violence under apartheid. In Mozambique the UNESCO-sponsored Culture of Peace Program seeks to use veterans as community peace promotors. In Cambodia the Thai Buddhist monastic order is providing technical assistance to revitalize *wats* and Buddhist temples, rekindling the moral authority and religiously rooted associational basis for civil society.

The most desirable outcome, for a country and its people, is the prevention of conflict. Where conflict has nonetheless occurred, the work of reconciliation has to be done. Reconciliation means bringing people to have faith again in civil institutions, in justice, and in the rule of law. In the final analysis, lasting reconciliation must be built on forgiveness.

Development Assistance at a Crossroads

Donors are increasingly seeking to establish early warning systems and rapid response mechanisms to forestall problems with DRPs, and to link relief and development efforts more closely if problems nonetheless arise. A major agenda item at the Halifax Summit of the Group of Seven industrial nations in June 1995 was to address ways of preventing and responding to crises. The Bretton Woods institutions and the United Nations were called on to reinvigorate coordination to facilitate a smoother transition from emergency to reconstruction, from war to peace.

Because most conflicts on the African continent cannot be viewed as purely local problems, multilateral institutions are often cast in a prominent role. Refugees who stream across borders to avoid devastation often turn local hostilities into regional conflicts and neighboring countries host warring armies for cross-border warfare. Zaire, Uganda, and Rwanda; the Sudan, Eritrea, and Uganda; and Liberia and Sierra Leone are home to just a few of the many regionally interlinked wars. Regional wars will end only when regional answers are found.

Reform of national military and security establishments, whether postconflict or in peacetime, is not within the purview of the multilateral institutions, nor do these institutions have a comparative advantage in this area. Moreover, the World Bank cannot by itself implement projects to rebuild social capital in war-torn societies. What the Bank can do is promote a secure and stable environment for development by supporting the removal and nonproliferation of mines and other antipersonnel weapons; encouraging the realignment of national public expenditures from nonproductive to productive sectors; assisting in the demobilization and reintegration of ex-combatants into a productive civilian life; financing the reconstruction of physical assets; and helping rebuild social capital. These are vital areas for Bank intellectual leadership, resource mobilization, and donor coordination.

Given the current political environment in Sub-Saharan Africa, the demand for such leadership will not diminish in the foreseeable future. On the contrary, more and more countries are appearing on the radar screen, from Sierra Leone and Liberia to Rwanda and Burundi to Angola and Chad. By honoring their requests for guidance, the Bank can lend credence to the role of a DRP as a central element in the reconstruction and development of war-torn societies and can play an important leadership role in the larger transition from war to peace.

Selected Bibliography

This bibliography lists selected publications on transitions from war to peace and on demobilization and reintegration. For detailed bibliographies on Ethiopia, Namibia, and Uganda, the reader is referred to Colletta and others (forthcoming).

Anthony, Ian, Pieter D. Wezeman, and Simeon T. Wezeman. 1995. "The Trade in Major Conventional Weapons." *SIPRI Yearbook 1995: Armaments, Disarmament and International Security.*

Azam, Jean-Paul, David Bevan, Paul Collier, Stefan Dercon, Jan Gunning, and Sanjay Pradhan. 1994. "Some Economic Consequences of the Transition from Civil War to Peace." Policy Research Working Paper 1392. World Bank, Policy Research Department, Washington, D.C.

Ball, Nicole, with Tammy Halevy. 1996. *Making Peace Work: The Role of the International Development Community.* Washington, D.C.: Overseas Development Council.

BICC (Bonn International Center for Conversion). 1995. "Demobilization in the Horn of Africa: Proceedings of the IRG Workshop, Addis Ababa, December 4–7." *BICC Brief* 4 (June). Bonn.

Brett, E. A. 1995. "Neutralising the Use of Force in Uganda: The Rôle of the Military in Politics." *Journal of Modern African Studies* 33(1):129–52.

Brzoka, Michael, Kees Kingma, and Herbert Wulf. 1995. "Demilitarization and Conversion." Paper prepared for the World Social Summit. Bonn International Center for Conversion.

Cilliers, Jakkie, ed. 1995. *Dismissed: Demobilization and Reintegration of Former Combatants in Africa.* Halfway House, South Africa: Institute for Defence Policy.

Cilliers, Jakkie, and Greg Mills, eds. 1995. *Peacekeeping in Africa.* Vol. 2. Halfway House, South Africa: Institute for Defence Policy.

Clark, Kimberly Mahling. 1996. "Fostering a Farewell to Arms: Preliminary Lessons Learned in the Demobilization and Reintegration of Ex-Combatants." U.S. Agency for International Development, Center for Development Information and Evaluation, Washington, D.C.

Colletta, Nat J. 1995. "From Warriors to Workers: The World Bank's Role in Post-Conflict Reconstruction." *Leaders* (October):204.

Colletta, Nat J., and Nicole Ball. 1993. "War to Peace Transition in Uganda." *Finance and Development* (June): 36–39.

Colletta, Nat J., Markus Kostner, and Ingo Wiederhofer, with assistance from Emilio Mondo, Taimi Sitari, and Tadesse A. Woldu. Forthcoming. *Case Studies in War-to-Peace Transition: The Demobilization and Reintegration of Ex-Combatants in Ethiopia, Namibia, and Uganda.* World Bank Discussion Paper 331. Washington, D.C.

Collier, Paul. 1995. "Civil War and the Economics of the Peace Dividend." WPS 95-8. Centre for the Study of African Economies, University of Oxford.

Creative Associates. 1995. "Country Experiences in Demobilization and Reintegration of Ex-Combatants. Workshop Proceedings and Case Study Findings." Washington, D.C.

Davies, Paul, with Nic Dunlop. 1994. *War of the Mines: Cambodia, Landmines, and the Impoverishment of a Nation.* Boulder, Colo.: Pluto Press.

George, Paul, Robert Bedeski, Bengt-Göran Bergstrand, Julian Cooper, and Evamaria Loose-Weintraub. 1995. "World Military Expenditure." *SIPRI Yearbook 1995: Armaments, Disarmament and International Security.*

German Development Institute. 1995. "Promoting the Reintegration of Former Female and Male Combatants in Eritrea." Draft final report. Berlin.

GTZ (Deutsche Gesellschaft für Technische Zusammenarbeit). 1992. "Proposal for the Reintegration of Refugees, Displaced Persons, and Ex-Combatants, with Special Reference to Sub-Sahara-Africa." Eschborn, Germany.

Holtzman, Steven. 1995. "Development Implications of Land Mines and Unexploded Ordnance." World Bank, Environment Department, Washington, D.C.

———. 1995. "Post-Conflict Reconstruction." Draft. World Bank, Environment Department, Washington, D.C.

Institute of Development Studies. 1994. "Linking Relief and Development." *IDS Bulletin* 25 (October). University of Sussex, Brighton, U.K.

Interafrica Group/NGO Networking Service. 1994. "Demobilization and Reintegration Issues in the Horn of Africa." Issues Note 2. Addis Ababa.

International Labour Office. 1995. "Reintegrating Demobilized Combatants: Experiences from Four African Countries." Paper prepared for the Expert Meeting on the Design of Guidelines for Training and Employment of Ex-Combatants, Harare, July 11–14. Geneva.

———. 1995. "The Reintegration of Young Ex-Combatants into Civilian Life." Paper prepared for the Expert Meeting on the Design of Guidelines for Training and Employment of Ex-Combatants, Harare, 11–14 July.

———. 1995. "Rehabilitation and Reintegration of Disabled Ex-Combatants." Paper prepared for the Expert Meeting on the Design of Guidelines for Training and Employment of Ex-Combatants, Harare, 11–14 July.

IRG (International Resource Group on Disarmament and Security in the Horn of Africa) and BICC (Bonn International Center for Conversion). 1995. "Report of the Seminar on Donor Response to Demobilization and Reintegration in the Horn of Africa." Bonn

Kingma, Kees. 1995. "On Civvy Street." *Life & Peace* (January), 18–20.

———. 1995. "Demobilization and Reintegration of Ex-Combatants: Critical Steps in the Peace Process." Draft chapter for *Jahrbuch Frieden 1996.* Bonn International Center for Conversion, Bonn, Germany.

Kingma, Kees, and Vanessa Sayers. 1995. "Demobilization in the Horn of Africa." Proceedings of the IRG Workshop, Addis Ababa, 4–7 December 1994. Bonn International Center for Conversion.

Knight, Malcolm, Norman Loayza, and Delano Villanueva. 1995. "The Peace Dividend: Military Spending Cuts and Economic Growth." International Monetary Fund, Washington, D.C.

Langseth, Peter, James Katorobo, E. Brett, and J. Munene, eds. 1995. *Uganda: Landmarks in Rebuilding a Nation*. Kampala: Fountain Publishers.

Ministry of Justice, South Africa. 1995. "Truth and Reconciliation Commission." Justice in Transition, Rondebosch.

Muscat, Robert J. 1995. "Conflict and Reconstruction: Roles for The World Bank." World Bank, Poverty and Social Policy Department, Washington, D.C.

Pereira da Silva, Luiz A., and Andrés Solimano. 1994. "The Transition and the Political Economy of Africa Socialist Countries at War (Angola and Mozambique)." World Bank, Africa–Southern Africa Department, Washington, D.C.

Refugee Policy Group and United Nations Department for Humanitarian Affairs. 1994. "Challenges of Demobilization and Reintegration: Background Paper and Conference Summary." New York.

Renner, Michael. 1994. "Budgeting for Disarmament: The Costs of War and Peace." Worldwatch Paper 122 (November). Worldwatch Institute, Washington, D.C.

Ross, Jacob, Simon Maxwell, and Margaret Buchanan-Smith. 1994. "Linking Relief to Development." Discussion Paper 344. Institute of Development Studies, University of Sussex, Brighton, U.K.

Scott, Colin. 1995. "Humanitarian Action and Security in Liberia: 1989-1994." Occasional Paper 20. Thomas J. Watson Jr. Institute for International Studies. Providence, R.I.

Sitari, Taimi, Julius Mtuleni, Lukas Nantanga, and Bruce Schimming. 1995. "Reintegration of Ex-Combatants in Namibia: Survey Report." ELCIN (Evangelical Lutheran Church in Namibia), Ondangwa.

Smock, David R. 1991. "Conflict Resolution in Africa: The Mediation of Africa's Wars." Prepared for the annual meeting of the American Political Science Association, August 29–September 1. American Political Science Association, Washington, D.C.

Srivastava, Ramesh. 1994. "Reintegrating Demobilized Combatants: A Report Exploring Options and Strategies for Training-Related Interventions." International Labour Office, Geneva.

United Nations. 1995. "Consolidated Inter-Agency Appeal: Angola." Revised Humanitarian Assistance Program for Demobilization and Reintegration, Department of Humanitarian Affairs.

UNDDSMS (United Nations Department for Development Support and Management Services). 1995. "International Colloquium on Post-Conflict Reconstruction Strategies." Held at the Austrian Study Centre for Peace and Conflict Resolution, Vienna, June 23–24. Vienna.

UNDP (United Nations Development Programme). n.d. "PRODERE: Human Development in Action." Office for Project Services, New York.

————. 1994. *Human Development Report*. New York: Oxford University Press.

UNESCO (United Nations Educational, Scientific, and Cultural Organization). 1995. "Culture of Peace: Promoting a Global Movement." Culture of Peace Program. Paris.

UNICEF (United Nations Children's Fund). 1996. "Children in War." In *The State of the World's Children 1996*. New York: Oxford University Press.

UNRISD (United Nations Research Institute for Social Development) and PSIS

(Programme for Strategic and International Security Studies. 1995. "The Challenge of Rebuilding War-torn Societies: Report on the Working Seminar at Cartigny, Geneva, 29 November to 1 December 1994." Geneva.

USACDA (United States Arms Control and Disarmament Agency.) 1995. *World Military Expenditures and Arms Transfers, 1993–1994.* Washington, D.C.

USAID (United States Agency for International Development). 1994. "Demobilization in Ethiopia: Lessons Learned." Addis Ababa.

U.S. Committee for Refugees. 1994. *World Refugee Survey.* Washington, D.C.

Weiss Fagen, Patricia, with Paula Uimonen 1995. "After the Conflict: A Review of Selected Sources on Rebuilding War-Torn Societies." War-torn Societies Project Occasional Paper 1. United Nations Research Institute for Social Development and Programme for Strategic and International Security Studies, Geneva.

Woldu, Tadesse A. 1995. "Ethiopia Ex-Combatant Reintegration Case Study: Results from the Field Study." Addis Abeba University.

World Bank. 1993. "Demobilization and Reintegration of Military Personnel in Africa: The Evidence from Seven Country Case Studies." Report IDP-130. Africa Regional Office, Washington D.C.

———. 1995. "The Demobilization and Reintegration of Ex-Combatants in Sub-Saharan Africa: Initiating Memorandum." Washington, D.C.

———. 1995a. "A Continent in Transition: Sub-Saharan Africa in the Mid-1990s." Discussion Paper. Africa Regional Office. Washington, D.C.

———. 1995b. "Status Report on Poverty in Sub-Saharan Africa 1995." Africa Technical Department, Human Resources and Poverty Division, Washington, D.C.

Directions in Development

Begun in 1994, this series contains short essays, written for a general audience, often to summarize published or forthcoming books or to highlight current development issues.

Africa's Management in the 1990s and Beyond: Reconciling Indigenous and Transplanted Institutions

Building Human Capital for Better Lives

Implementing Projects for the Poor: What Has Been Learned?

India's Family Welfare Program: Moving to a Reproductive and Child Health Approach (with a separate supplement)

Investing in People: The World Bank in Action (also available in French and Spanish)

Managing Commodity Booms—and Busts

Meeting the Infrastructure Challenge in Latin America and the Caribbean (also available in Spanish)

Nurturing Development: Aid and Cooperation in Today's Changing World

Private and Public Initiatives: Working Together for Health and Education

Private Sector Participation in Water Supply and Sanitation in Latin America

Reversing the Spiral: The Population, Agriculture, and Environment Nexus in Sub-Saharan Africa (with a separate supplement)

Taxing Bads by Taxing Goods: Pollution Control with Presumptive Charges

Toward Sustainable Management of Water Resources

Trade Performance and Policy in the New Independent States

Unshackling the Private Sector: A Latin American Story

The Uruguay Round: Widening and Deepening the World Trading System

Water Supply, Sanitation, and Environmental Sustainability: The Financing Challenge